PUB WA
IN KEN

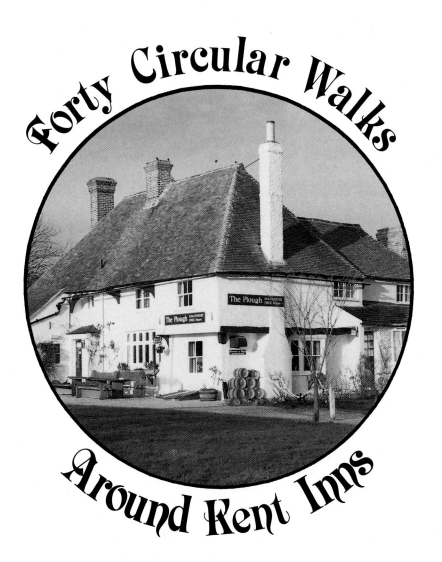

Forty Circular Walks

Around Kent Inns

David Hancock

Other publications in the series
"Pub Walks in Dorset"
"Forty More Pub Walks in Dorset"
"Pub Walks in Hampshire & the I.O.W."
"Pub Walks in West Sussex"
"Pub Walks in East Sussex"
"Pub Walks in Devon"
"Pub Walks in Cornwall"

1st Edition – published May 1994.

ACKNOWLEDGEMENTS
In researching this collection of walks I am indebted to the contribution of my friend and colleague Bonita Toms who not only accompanied me on all the walks, but took the photographs and made many invaluable observations and notes on each walk.

Bonita and I would like to thank our close friends David and Sandra Boys and family in Marden and my parents, Derek and Evelyn Hancock in Maidstone, for their generous hospitality and support, and for putting up with us on our frequent visits to Kent. I am also grateful to my parents for checking in detail three of the walks.

I acknowledge the co-operation of all the landlords of the pubs included, for providing the essential information needed and for their enthusiasm in the concept of Pub Walks. Lastly, I thank Mike Power for entrusting me with this project.

© M. Power Publications 1994

ISBN 1 898073 03 1

Publishers Note
Whilst every care has been taken to ensure that all the information given in this book is correct, errors will occur due to many factors. Paths can be re-routed, stiles can sometimes replace gates and even the pubs themselves change hands. Neither the publishers nor the printers can accept responsibility for any inaccuracies.

Power Publications
1 Clayford Avenue, Ferndown
Dorset BH22 9PQ

Front cover: The Plough, Stalisfield Green
Photo and book photos: Bonita Toms
Printed by Pardy & Son (Printers) Ltd., Ringwood, Hampshire

INTRODUCTION

This collection of 40 circular walks explores deep into the heart of the beautiful Kentish countryside – The Garden of England – and discovers a diverse landscape with a rich heritage. The chalk escarpment and rolling downland of the North Downs and the fertile slopes of the greensand ridge characterise the high points of the county, the latter providing panoramic views across the level, sheep-grazed pastures of the Weald to the undulating ridges of the High Weald and the Sussex border. Kent's coastal scenery is just as varied, ranging from the spectacular white cliffs of Dover with views of France to wild and desolate marshland along the estuaries of the Swale, Medway and Thames.

Dotted across this delightful patchwork quilt of hop fields, orchards, woodland and pasture are the ubiquitous oast-houses, fine medieval manor houses and a wealth of unspoilt villages that preserve ancient black and white timbered, weatherboarded or tile-hung cottages, picturesque churches and an excellent choice of traditional inns. After travelling the length and breadth of the county, exploring numerous historic village inns and many splendid hostelries tucked away well off the beaten track, I have selected forty for inclusion, either for their charm and character, their peaceful location or for the vicinity of scenic and interesting walks. No charge has been made for the pub's inclusion in this guide.

Kent is blessed with a superb network of well waymarked and well maintained footpaths, thanks to the efforts of the County Council and the popularity of this leisure activity in the county. Four long distance footpaths – North Downs Way/Pilgrims Way, Greensand Way, Wealdway, Saxon Shore Way – cross the county and many of the walks in this guide incorporate sections of these scenic trails. The walks are all circular, ranging between 2 miles to 7 miles in length and as well as a detailed route description and sketch map, there are pointers to places of interest on the route or nearby. The walks are fairly short in order to appeal to families and are planned to start and finish at the pub, although it is possible to start anywhere along the route. If you are planning to park your car at the pub it is only courteous to ask the landlord's permission first.

It is advisable to take with you the appropriate Ordnance Survey map which is indicated at the beginning of each walk, along with the exact reference of the start point. The map number refers to the 1:50,000 – $1\frac{1}{4}$ inch to the mile – Landranger series and the maps required for Kent are Nos. 177, 178, 179, 188 and 189. For more detailed maps there is also the Pathfinder series which cover an area 1:25,000 – $2\frac{1}{2}$ inches to the mile. If you should find any of the paths obstructed in any way please inform the Public Rights of Way Manager, Highways and Transport Department, Kent County Council, Springfield, Maidstone, Kent, ME14 2LX. Telephone: 0622 696740.

Walking is extremely good for you and the best way to explore the countryside, but a few simple rules must be observed when undertaking any of these walks. Try to wear suitable clothing that befits the season and weather conditions. A good idea is to take a pair of lightweight trousers or leggings with you in summer, especially if you are wearing shorts, as many paths become overgrown with nettles and thistles. A walking stick is also ideal for clearing such painful obstructions and for testing the stability of the ground ahead. Waterproof walking boots or stout, well-treaded shoes are strongly recommended during the winter as trails are often very wet and muddy. Other handy items are a compass and if walking late into the evening, a torch. Take care on country lanes without pavements.

Wherever you go always remember the country code. Guard against all fires, fasten all gates, keep dogs under control and always on a lead where there is livestock, keep to the path across farmland, take all litter home, respect wildlife and do not pick flowers.

Finally, I hope you enjoy these walks and the hospitality and individual charm of all the pubs as much as I did during my research.

David Hancock

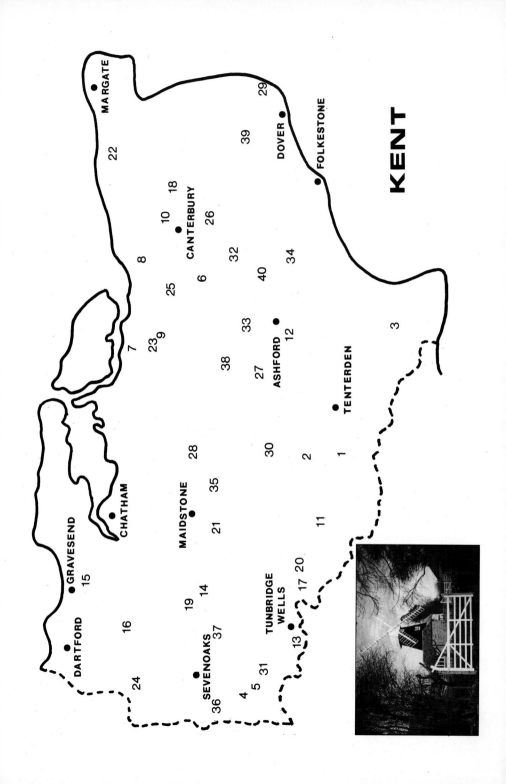

KENT

MARGATE
22
29
DOVER
39
FOLKESTONE
18
10
CANTERBURY
26
8
32
25 6
34
40
23 9
7
33
38
ASHFORD
27 12
TENTERDEN
3
28
30
2
1
CHATHAM
MAIDSTONE
35
21
11
GRAVESEND
15
20
DARTFORD
16
14
19
17
TUNBRIDGE
WELLS
SEVENOAKS
37
13
24
36
4
5 31

Tourist Information Centres

For further information on places to visit mentioned on each walk contact the following offices:

Ashford	0233 629165	Maidstone	0622 673581
Canterbury	0227 766567	New Romney	0679 64044 (summer only)
Cranbrook	5080 712538 (summer only)	Sevenoaks	0732 450305
Dartford	0322 343243	Tenterden	05806 3572 (summer only)
Dover	0304 205108	Tonbridge	0732 770929
Faversham	0795 534542	Tunbridge Wells	0892 515675
Gravesend	0474 337600	Whitstable	0227 275482
Herne Bay	0227 361911		

The King William VI, Benenden

Located in the heart of the village, close to its large attractive green complete with cricket pitch and church is the King William IV, an excellent unspoilt village local that dates back to the 16th century and boasts an intriguing history. It was originally a chapel, providing a resting place for weary pilgrims on their way to Canterbury. On acquiring its license in the 18th century it soon became one of the haunts of the infamous Hawkhurst gang, a wild band of smugglers that terrorised the area. Nowadays, the two character bars are frequented by a pleasant mix of locals and well-heeled diners. The relaxing, upmarket rustic in style lounge bar boasts a huge inglenook fireplace with log fire and seating, exposed beams and is furnished with honey pine tables, some cricket tables, pews and farmhouse kitchen tables. By contrast, the splendidly traditional public bar is smaller and more basic with exposed floorboards. Owned by Shepherd Neame the pub is personally run by Alan Austin.

Cask ales served on handpump are Shepherd Neame Master Brew and Spitfire with the addition of two stronger brews - Bishops Finger and Porter - during the winter months.

A short, daily-changing blackboard menu lists the home-cooked selection of food, which may include beef and vegetable soup, duck and liver pâté, smoked salmon mousse and Stilton and pears on toast for starters, followed by Stilton and celery quiche, cottage pie, macaroni cheese, salmon and broccoli bake, rabbit casserole, chicken wellington and steak and mushroom pie. Good snacks range from filled rolls, sandwiches and jacket potatoes to ploughmans and home-made burgers. Bar food is served daily between 12 noon and 2pm and 7pm till 9pm Wednesday to Saturday only.

Weekday opening times are 11am till 2.30pm and 6pm till 11pm and all day on summer Saturdays.

Children are welcome in part of the lounge bar and dogs are allowed in on a lead, except on Sundays.

Telephone: (0580) 240636.

Village and pub are located on the B2086 between Rolvenden and Cranbrook, 5 miles west of Tenterden.

Approx. distance of walk: 4½ miles. O.S. Map No. 188 TQ 808/329

Parking is limited at the inn, but there is space by the village green near the church.

A delightfully varied, undulating and scenic walk along well waymarked field paths and woodland tracks in a very unspoilt rural part of Kent. The going can be wet and muddy after rain especially beside some of the small brooks, so good waterproof footwear is essential during the winter. Of interest nearby is the fascinating collection of historic vehicles at Rolvenden.

1. Turn right on leaving the pub, then right again beside the village green to the church. Bear right with the footpath fingerpost, then keep left along the metalled pathway and descend via three wooden gates to a road. Keep left along the verge, then shortly climb the stile beside the driveway to Woodside. Head half-right on a defined path across a field to an arrowed stile preceeding woodland. Follow a good path to a junction of tracks and cross straight over onto a wide track through the wood. Keep ahead where the track bears sharp right and follow footpath 333 downhill to a stile on the woodland edge. Proceed along the right-hand edge of a field, parallel to a brook and soon climb a stile by a gate onto a lane.

2. Turn left, then keep right at a T-junction and shortly bear off left uphill along a T-road. Pass Barnhill Cottage, then lookout for a waymarked stile on your left beside a gate. Proceed straight ahead uphill across pasture and pass through a yellow marked field gate near a house. Continue along the field edge, pass through a further gate and maintain direction to a metal gate in the field corner. Bear right into Ramsden Farm, keep ahead across the crossroads of concrete farm tracks, then curve right behind a barn and turn left with yellow waymarker

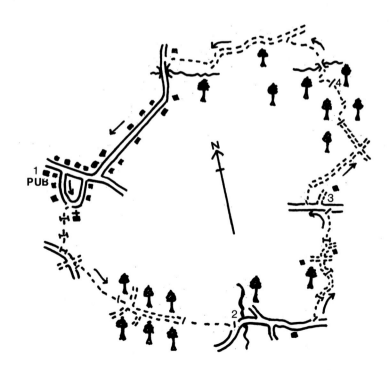

on telegraph pole to a gate. Proceed half-right towards a disused windmill, soon to pick up the grassy path in the field corner that leads to a stile and the B2086, near the old windmill.

3. Turn left, then in a little way cross the road and a waymarked stile beside a driveway. Bear slightly right towards a line of poplar trees and climb a stile into an orchard. Turn right along its edge, shortly to bear right with yellow markers through a gateway into the adjacent field. Keep left along the grassy field edge then at a crossing of tracks turn left with an arrow along the left-hand edge of an orchard and downhill into coniferous woodland, eventually reaching a stile. Follow the grassy track which curves right to a further gate and stile and resume your route through woodland.

4. Climb a stile on the woodland fringe, bear left then right downhill and shortly cross a footbridge over a stream. Keep left, cross a stile, then turn left uphill along the edge of a field to waymarked stile in the hedge and turn left along a wide established trackway. Remain on this track, skirting ponds and woodland, then parallel with a stream - your route can be very wet and muddy - to a narrow lane. Turn left and follow it into Benenden, turning right at the B-road in the village back to the pub.

Rolvenden Mill on the B2086 between Benenden and Rolvenden

The Three Chimneys, Biddenden

This real gem of a country pub has been my personal favourite in Kent for many years. Dating from 1420, it was originally a half-timbered farmhouse before becoming an ale house during the 1800's to serve the workers on the neighbouring hop picking farms. The unusual pub name relates to its location rather than to the number of chimneys on the building, as it is a corruption of the French 'trois chemins' or 'the three ways'. During the Napoleonic Wars, French officers were held prisoners at nearby Sissinghurst Castle, but were allowed to go for country walks and the junction of the three roads where the pub stands was their parole limit - hence the name. The unassuming facade hides a classic interior that has been virtually untouched over the centuries. A warren of rooms radiate off the central bar and feature a wealth of low beams, flagstone floors and wood-panelled walls.

The atmosphere is warm, welcoming and traditional with a delightful mix of rustic old furniture - wooden pews and benches, sturdy tables - blazing winter log fires and evening candlelight. The small, splendidly traditional public bar is dominated by a vast inglenook fireplace and heavy, head-cracking beams. The only 'modern' addition to the pub is the rear Garden Room, which is furnished with a collection of old-fashioned tables and chairs and blends in well with its adjacent older bars. It overlooks the large shrub and bench-filled garden.

This excellent free house dispenses seven real ales tapped straight from the cask - Adnams Best Bitter, Fremlins Bitter, Brakspear Bitter, Marstons Pedigree, Morland Old Speckled Hen, Wadworth 6X, Harveys Old Ale - as well as the heady Biddenden farm cider and an interesting list of wines.

The imaginative range of decent home-cooked food is listed on daily-changing blackboard menus dotted around the pub. A typical selection may include carrot and orange soup, buttered haddock pâté, duck or chestnut mousse, followed by beef and pigeon casserole, partridge and apricot pie, steak and oyster pie, Kentish lamb pie, and vegetarian choices, such as aubergine and tomato pie and vegetable goulash. Good puddings include date and walnut pudding and gooseberry and elderflower tart.

Weekday opening times are from 11am till 2.30pm and 6pm till 11pm.

Children are welcome in the Garden Room and dogs are allowed in on leads.

Telephone: (0580) 291472.

9

Walk No. 2

Pub is located just off the A262 between Biddenden and Sissinghurst, 1 mile west of Biddenden.

Approx. distance of walk: 4 miles. O.S. Map No. 188 TQ 827/388

There is a large car park to the front of the inn.

An enjoyable level walk along established tracks, peaceful country lanes and field paths with the opportunity to visit the splendid colourful gardens of Sissinghurst Castle (NT). The Tudor mansion and gardens were restored by Sir Harold Nicholson and the writer Vita Sackville-West and are a delight to explore in both spring and summer (open April to mid-October). Some of the tracks can be very wet and muddy during the winter months. Further attractions in the locality include the attractive weatherboarded village of Cranbrook with its fine working 'smock mill' (open). The small town of Tenterden is closeby and is the beginning of the Kent and East Sussex Railway, a delightful 7-mile steam journey through the Weald.

1. Leave the pub car park at the exit by the pub sign and turn right along the narrow lane. Keep left on reaching a junction, pass the entrance to Bettenham Manor, then where the lane curves right, bear off left beside a metal barrier onto a wide trackway. Gently descend and cross the bridge across Hammer Stream and continue towards Sissinghurst Castle.

2. On reaching the complex of buildings with the shop/barn in front of you, bear left, then right with restaurant to your right and follow the metalled track past the Farm Shop onto a driveway towards a house. At the house turn sharp right onto an established tree-lined pathway - can be very wet and muddy - and gently descend, eventually reaching a track beside a house. Follow the driveway to a junction of lanes.

3. Proceed straight across, waymarked Sand Lane, then just beyond metal barns (Brissenden Farm) on your left, pass through green double gates to the right onto a concrete drive. Pass a barn, then bear half-right onto a worn path across a field to a stile in a hedge. Continue across pasture to a further stile beside a tree, then proceed ahead to cross a footbridge over a stream. Keep left along the field edge, cross a plank bridge in the field corner and turn right onto a wide grassy path. Where the track curves right cross the waymarked footbridge ahead, then pass through scrub and follow the worn path to a stile and a lane. Climb the stile opposite, step over a covered wire fence and follow it left-handed, shortly to bear slightly right to a stile. Maintain direction behind bungalows to a further stile and turn left along the lane back to the pub.

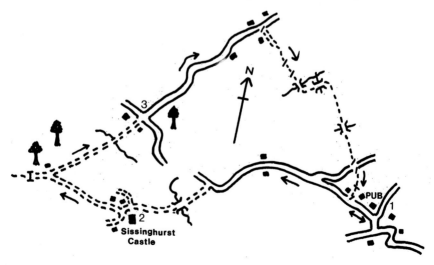

10

The Woolpack, Brookland

Originally a beacon keepers cottage dating from 1410, this low, white-painted pub is tucked away along a lane, isolated among open sheep pastures and overlooking a reed-fringed dyke. It has been a pub for over 400 years and was a well known smuggling haunt when gangs would use the Romney Marsh coast to trade wool for rum and brandy brought over from France. The pub has featured in many films as a smugglers inn. Beyond the old worn brick entrance and extremely low doorway lies the splendid main bar, which oozes atmosphere and charm. A roaring winter log fire burns in the massive inglenook which has side seating for those frozen to the bone and a head-cracking low beamed ceiling awaits unsuspecting customers. A quarry-tiled floor is topped with rustic benches, long tables and a mix of stools, wheelback chairs and pub tables. A collection of water jugs hangs above the bar and various pieces of copper and brass adorn the walls. Adjacent simply furnished games bar with pool, darts, shove ha'penny, spinning jenny to play and a central open brick fireplace.

Licensee John Palmer maintains this Shepherd Neame pub and dispenses well conditioned Master Brew, Spitfire and either their Best Bitter or Porter on handpump. Summer sipping can be enjoyed in the waterside garden, complete with free-range geese and ducks.

Bar food is served daily between 12 noon and 2pm and from 6pm till 9pm. The short selection of good value, home-cooked dishes include soup and crusty bread, shepherds pie, lasagne and salad, chilli, steak pie, Dover sole, mixed grill, rump steak, cod and chips, pork chops, chips and peas and vegetable au gratin. A daily special board may feature a warming casserole, liver and bacon or a roast. Good walkers snacks include a range of ploughmans, sandwiches, filled jacket potatoes and garlic bread.

Weekday opening times are from 11am till 2.30pm and 6pm till 11pm.

Children are most welcome in the games bar, but dogs are not allowed inside. Telephone: (0797) 344321.

Walk No. 3

Brookland is located on the A259 New Romney to Rye road on the Romney Marsh. The pub lies 1 mile south-west of the village towards Rye, just off the A259.

Approx. distance of walk: 3½ miles. O.S. Map No. 189 TQ 978/245

There is a car park at the pub and space alongside the lane.

A short level stroll through sheep filled pastures, open arable fields, across dykes and along quiet narrow lanes. Due to the low lying nature of the land it can be wet underfoot and the cultivated land hard going, especially if recently ploughed. The splendid ancient church of Saint Augustine in Brookland, with its curious wooden belfry, is one of the most attractive and interesting churches in Romney Marsh and is the focus of this walk.

1. Leave the pub, turn left along the lane across the dyke and shortly bear off left with fingerpost and drop down into pasture. Climb the metal gate, then bear diagonally right through pasture, crossing a dyke soon to reach a stile and lane close to an isolated cottage. Turn right, then in a few yards climb the waymarked stile left and keep to the left-hand field edge to a wooden footbridge. Continue across an open field to a stile and bear half-left across a further field to a stile in the far corner and enter a paddock. Proceed left-handed in front of a cottage to a stile and continue to a swing gate onto a lane. Turn right, following the lane left to visit the unusual historic church of St Augustine in Brookland village.

2. Retrace steps across the paddocks, your path waymarked to Fairfield. Beyond the second stile bear right into a grassy field and keep to its left-hand edge, passing an old white shed. On reaching the field corner, bear half-right across open crop field to a fingerpost, a stile and the A-road. Turn left and soon cross over to take the arrowed, well defined path that heads half-left across an open field and through a gateway to reach a footbridge over a dyke.

3. Beyond the dyke turn left along the field edge, ignore the arrowed path right and continue to a stile and lane. Turn right and remain on the lane as it bears left, soon to pass The Laurels and a farm complex to a T-junction of lanes. Turn left and follow the lane with good open views to the main road. Taking great care, turn right along the road to a sharp right-hand bend, then bear off left along a lane for the short distance back to the pub.

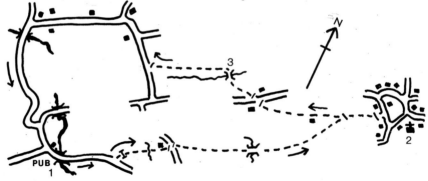

Key to Symbols

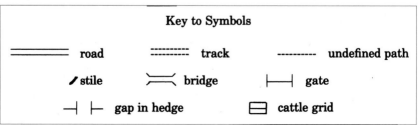

road ⠀⠀⠀ track ⠀⠀⠀ undefined path

✓ stile ⠀⠀⠀ bridge ⠀⠀⠀ gate

gap in hedge ⠀⠀⠀ cattle grid

Warming winter log fire in The Woolpack

The interesting church of St. Augustine in Brookland

The Castle Inn, Chiddingstone

Located opposite the parish church in a unique, unspoilt row of Tudor timbered houses, this historic tile-hung inn with its leaded casement windows and projecting gables is, like the rest of the village, owned by the National Trust. This magnificent building is first referred to in 1420 and was then known as Waterslip House. It was bought in 1712 by Thomas Weller, a tailor, who with his brother started the inn about 1730 and some 260 years later it is still one of the main centres of village life and an extremely popular refreshment stop for visiting tourists. Despite its popularity, this fine inn has remained delightfully untouched over the years, comprising two traditional and atmospheric bars. The classic public bar is splendidly rustic with a black and terracotta chequered quarry-tiled floor - no problem with muddy boots - a heavily beamed ceiling, an old brick fireplace with woodburner and simple wall bench seating. It is a true locals bar. Those seeking extra comfort can relax in the cosy, beamed and carpeted saloon bar. Sunny summer days can be enjoyed on the vine-covered terrace and in the pretty rear garden, complete with small pool, fountain, flower borders and a neat bench-filled lawn. The pub is a free house and has been personally run by the Lucas family since 1964.

The well stocked bar dispenses Shepherd Neame Master Brew, Harveys Sussex Bitter and the 'local' Larkins Sovereign Bitter on handpump, as well as a range of 30 malt whiskies and a choice of over 150 wines from a wide-ranging list.

Good bar food is served all week, the printed menu listing sound favourites like filled jacket potatoes, open sandwiches, ploughmans, home-made pâtés and soups, chilli, beef and vegetable curry and a selection of salads. A short blackboard menu highlights the daily dishes which may include leek and potato soup, moules mariniere and a pasta dish. Puddings range from Dutch apple slice and cheesecake to speciality ice-creams. A set fireside menu is also available in the bar.

Weekday opening times are from 10.30am till 3pm and 6pm till 11pm (Saturday 10.30am till 11pm).

Both children and dogs are welcome inside.

Telephone: (0892) 870247.

Village is situated 1 mile south of the B2027 Penshurst to Edenbridge road.

Approx. distance of walk: 5½ miles. O.S. Map No. 188 TQ 500/452

Parking is limited at the pub to spaces along the village lane.

A most enjoyable fairly level ramble, affording good countryside views making an ideal walk for the whole family. Part of the walk passes through the grounds of Hever Castle, an enchanting, double-moated, 13th-century castle that was the childhood home of Anne Boleyn (open daily mid March to early November). Also open to the public (April to October) is Chiddingstone Castle, a 17th-century house displaying fine paintings and Egyptian and Oriental antiquities.

1. From the inn turn right along the lane and take the first footpath right if wishing to see the 'Chiding Stone' - legend has it that the stone was a natural platform for a preacher to address his followers. The main route follows the second path left, just beyond a driveway. Proceed across two stiles into a field, then drop down to a stile by a copse directly ahead. Keep to the right and pass through the copse to an open pasture. Cross a track, then a stile on the right and follow the path through a farm complex to meet the farm road, which bears right between cottages.

2. Turn left into a private road (vehicles only), go through a small gate on the right to join a fenced track. Continue along the track soon to cross a stile located between two large steel gates and enter woodland. Follow track downhill, cross a footbridge over a stream, waymarked Eden Valley Walk and proceed with markers over a stile and along a fenced track to a further stile and road. Cross over and keep to the footpath soon to pass to the right of a farm and houses, eventually reaching the drive to

Hever Castle. Go through the gate on the right, follow the drive then the footpath over a footbridge to another fenced path and shortly pass through Hever churchyard to the road.

3. Turn left, then where the road veers sharp right, keep straight on to pass the school and join a footpath which leads you to a road. Turn left, then in a few yards climb the waymarked stile right and proceed to the left-hand corner of the field by a pond and cross two stiles into the adjacent field. Keep left, climb two further stiles and head for the stile in the right-hand corner of the field to a road. Turn right, then left at a T-junction and soon take the next lane left, eventually reaching a T-junction opposite Wilderness Farm.

4. Turn right, then on reaching a 'give way' sign, climb the stile on the left onto a track. Follow this established track through woodland with several iron gates to join a fenced track (good views). On reaching an iron gate and stile by the private drive used on the outward route, turn right and retrace your steps back to the Castle Inn.

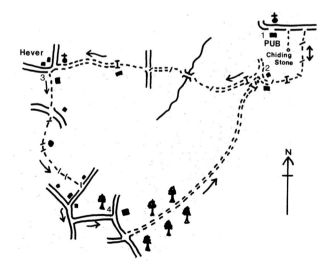

The Rock Inn, Chiddingstone Hoath

Hidden away in the depths of unspoilt countryside, this attractive, creeper and rose adorned brick and tile-hung building dates back to 1510. For many years it was part of the Hever estate and has been used as a slaughter house, among other things, before becoming an ale house serving the estate workers. Old world character and charm fills the unadultered main bar which boasts a low, oak beamed ceiling, an original uneven red-brick floor - no problem with muddy boots - exposed wall beams, leaded windows and a splendid inglenook with roaring woodburner. Old wooden casks serve as tables and seating includes tapestry covered stools, padded bench seats and a comfortable worn leather chair which fronts the fire. Above this chair and mounted on the wall is a huge, menacing bull's head, the object of a local pub game, Ringing the Bull. Cream painted walls are hung with several prints and a collection of banknotes decorate the heavy beams. The adjacent, smaller and cosier bar is furnished with old church wall pews and red leatherette chairs and has a small brick fireplace. Since 1990 this rustic pub has been a free house and is personally run by Richard Shaw-Kew.

Two unusual wooden beer engines dispense Kentish ales, namely Shepherd Neame Master Brew Bitter and the local Larkins Bitter which is brewed a mile or so down the lane. Secluded rear garden with picnic benches for fair weather days.

Home-cooked bar food is listed on a blackboard menu above the bar and features daily-changing dishes as well as sound favourites, which remain chalked up. Choices include vegetable soup, Ardennes pâté, potted shrimps, 4 types of ploughmans, lasagne, beef casserole, cottage pie, macaroni cheese, whole plaice on the bone, steak and kidney pie and winter game from local shoots. Separate sandwich board. Home-made puddings may include treacle tart, apple crumble and various sponges. Food is available between 12 noon and 2.30pm and from 6.30pm till 10pm, except Wednesday evenings. No hot food Sunday lunchtimes.

Weekday opening times are from 11.30am till 3pm and from 5.30pm till 11pm.

Children are not encouraged as space is limited, but the garden is fenced and safe. Dogs are very welcome inside.

Telephone: (0892) 870296.

The pub is located at Hoath Corner between Chiddingstone and Hoath Corner, 3 miles west of Penshurst.

Approx. distance of walk: 4½ miles. O.S. Map No. 188 TQ 498/431

There is a small car park at the pub.

A most enjoyable, scenic rural ramble along good paths, including the Sussex Border Path, and along short stretches of quiet country lanes. Generally easy going.

1. From the pub turn left, then almost immediately right at a junction to join a narrow lane, passing Truggers Farms and shortly reach a T-junction. Cross over and pass through a waymarked metal gate onto a track beside a house. On reaching a metal gate climb the stile on the right into pasture and bear diagonally left downhill to a stile on the woodland fringe. Follow the narrow path along the woodland edge and shortly bear right into the wood, downhill to a footbridge over a stream. Climb a muddy bank to a stile, (path 534), enter pasture, keep left-handed beside woodland, then keep ahead at the end of the trees, uphill to a stile in the hedgerow.
2. Continue ahead, pass in front of cottages, bear left along driveway to cross a stile beside a gate and proceed downhill to a T-junction of tracks. Turn left, shortly pass Wickens Farm and bear right (yellow arrow, path 675) off the farm track to a waymarked stile. Follow narrow defined path beside wire fence to a fence stile, then bear half-left across pasture to a further stile and continue along arrowed trackway, downhill through Sandfields Farm to a lane. Keep left across the railway, pass Orchard Cottage, and shortly climb waymarked stile on your left, just before Moat Farm.
3. Proceed round a pond, keep right-hand through pasture to a small wooden gate and footbridge over a stream. Cross over and turn immediately left across a stile to join the well worn Sussex Border Path, parallel to the stream. Continue across three pastures via stiles and a footbridge, then walk beside railway embankment, shortly to pass through a gate on the left and go under the railway. Bear half-right across meadow, over plank bridge to a stile near a footbridge with padlocked gate. Climb the stile, bear left to and cross further footbridge over the stream. Leave Border Path, (arrowed right), keep straight ahead across meadow to a stile beside a pole fence, then cut the corner of a field to a further stile and proceed to the right of a barn and timbered house to a stile and bear right along driveway to a lane.
4. Turn left, cross stream, then turn right through a gate onto a track and shortly bear off right with green arrow on tree to a metal gate. Head uphill, keep left of tree-ringed hollow to a stile and continue straight on to a further stile beside a horse jump. Soon bear right with the wide gallop, cross stile on the left and keep right-handed along field edge and around a pond to an arrowed stile and junction of paths. Climb the stile, keep right-handed along hedge to a further stile and a lane. Cross stile opposite and follow narrow path gently uphill beside fencing and driveway through scrub area to a stile. Keep ahead on grassy path between crop fields soon to bear right to a lane. Turn left and follow the lane back to the pub.

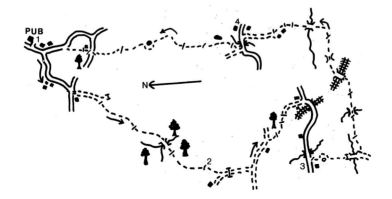

17

The White Horse, Chilham

This attractive white painted, part-timbered pub nestles in the corner of the one of prettiest village squares in Kent and must claim to be the most photographed hostelry in the county. Built in 1422 as a thatched farm dwelling and later becoming an ale house used for festivals held at the adjacent church, it is, like the rest of the village, steeped in history. Refurbishments in 1956 revealed the skeletons of two men, possibly soldiers that were killed at the Battle of Chilham during the Wat Tyler rebellion of 1380. They are now buried in the churchyard. Also uncovered was the massive inglenook which was hidden by brick for over 200 years and displays a Lancastrian rose carved at the end of its mantelbeam - a relic of the War of the Roses. The welcoming interior is open-plan in style, spreading around a central bar servery and features a carved beamed ceiling, some standing timbers, good winter log fires, comfortable sofas and darkwood tables and chairs. Attractive prints, paintings and local photographs adorn the walls and an unusual collection of handbells hang from the ceiling in the food servery area. There is a pleasant walled garden, shaded by cherry trees and overlooks a village lane, cottages and the churchyard.

Roy Terry efficiently manages this extremely busy Whitbread Wayside Inn and his well-stocked bar dispenses Fremlins Bitter, Flowers Original, Fullers London Pride, Brakspear Bitter and a guest ale on handpump, as well as a fine selection of fruit wines from the Chilham vineyard and local pure apple juice.

Bar food is available from 12 noon till 2.30pm (4pm in summer) and from 7pm till 9pm (10pm Friday and Saturday). Food is not served Tuesday evenings in winter as this is the regular quiz night. The printed lunchtime snack menu lists a home-made soup, salads, country platters and a range of sandwiches, while evening fare ranges from grilled trout, lemon sole bonne femme to venison in red wine and a selection of grills and steaks. Daily-changing specials are written on a board above the bar and may include sausage casserole, sweet and sour turkey, macaroni cheese, vegetable lasagne and vegetable and lentil crumble.

Weekday opening times are from 11am till 11pm.

Due to limited space children are not allowed in the bar.

Telephone: (0227) 730355.

Village lies just off the A28 and A252, 4 miles south-west of Canterbury.

Approx distance of walk: 5 miles. O.S. Map No. 179 TR 068/536.

Park in village square or in the large free car park at the bottom of the village, off the A252.

A delightful, gently undulating walk starting from one of Kent's most attractive villages, complete with fine castle grounds and raptor collection (open April to mid-October). It explores the scenic well waymarked tracks and woodland paths in the Stour Valley and is generally easy going, but the woodland ways can be muddy.

1. From the pub turn left and leave the square, heading down the The Street past the post office. Keep left at a junction by the Woolpack, then bear right with the lane to the A28. Cross over onto a lane beside Ashford Road Service Station and join the Stour Valley Walk. Cross the level crossing, then the River Stour and pass to the right of Chilham Mill. Cross a stile and a further river channel, then bear left to join the narrow path beside the river. At a crossroads of paths, proceed straight across, then keep left around a field edge, gently climbing to a stile and a track.
2. Turn left, (good views along Stour Valley), ignore stile and waymarkers on your right and remain on the trackway to a metalled lane. Turn immediately right onto a waymarked path along the driveway to Mystole Farm. Pass the entrance to Mystole Court and turn right onto a gravel track towards farm buildings. Keep right at a fork and follow grass centred track uphill. On reaching a yellow topped post bear off right along the left-hand side of a fence, through a hedgerow, then along a track into a mixed woodland.
3. Bear left to a T-junction of tracks, turn left, then immediately right onto a narrow

path waymarked with blue markers. Turn right at the next junction and follow this established path to the woodland fringe. Follow blue arrow along left-hand edge of an open field, soon to leave woodland edge on a defined grassy path between fields. At a marker post with arrows, bear right onto a wide track, shortly to bear right again to a stile preceeding woodland. Descend on a narrow path, keeping ahead at a crossroads of tracks, your path becoming hedged with good cameo views. Proceed straight on at a fork of paths, cross a stile and keep right downhill to merge with a track.
4. Bear right, pass beneath the railway, cross a stile beside a gate and follow driveway through farm complex to the main road. Turn left along the grass verge, shortly to cross over to a waymarked gate. Cross the footbridge over the Stour and bear diagonally right along a defined path across pasture. Cross a stile in the hedge on the left and head half-right across an open field to a fingerpost by some trees and join a narrow path to a lane opposite Orchard House. Turn right (North Downs Way) and follow it around the grounds of Chilham Castle, then up School Hill back into Chilham Square.

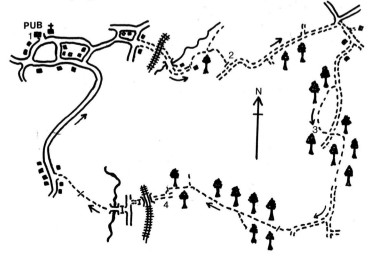

19

The Ship, Conyer Quay

Built in 1642, the Ship has been in its time a bakers shop, a blacksmiths and on becoming an alehouse in the 18th century, a notable smugglers haunt. Located beside Conyer Creek, its shingle-covered front terrace overlooks a working waterfront and open marshland. Inside, a real quayside atmosphere pervades in the rambling and comfortable rooms, which have wooden floors, planked ceilings and walls hung with fishing nets, maps and other nautical memorabilia. An assortment of furniture includes darkwood tables, captains chairs, stools and various church pews and benches. Shelves of used books are sold or exchanged with the proceeds going to charity and customers are welcome to peruse the library of local books on show. Also available are a variety of board and card games as well as the traditional games of shove ha'penny, cribbage and dominoes. The adjacent Smugglers restaurant is gloomy, candle-lit and atmospheric.

The Ship's main claim to fame is the quite remarkable range of drinks that landlord Alec Heard dispenses from behind the bar - supposedly the greatest selection than any other pub in Britain. Five handpumps have pulled through over 250 different real ales in the past year and twice yearly the pub hosts successful beer festivals. The mind-boggling drinks list extends to Biddenden farm cider, 8 lagers, imported draught beers, over 250 whiskies, 150 liquers, 25 rums, 50 brandies and some 200 global wines, a hundred of which are available by the glass. 'Happy hour' is from 6-7pm Monday to Friday and 7-8pm on Sundays.

The comprehensive printed menu lists snacks such as toasted sandwiches, farmhouse soup, ploughmans, lasagne, curries, home-made steak and kidney pie and vegetarian choices like broccoli and almond lasagne and spicy samosas. The popular Smugglers Restaurant á la carte menu features over 50 dishes including a range of steaks, salad bar platters, rack of lamb and roast chicken with fresh vegetables. Seafood dishes are the restaurants speciality, notably the fresh oysters, moules mariniere, dressed crab and fresh lobster (24 hours notice).

Weekday opening times are from 11am till 3pm and 6pm till 11pm.

Children are welcome in the restaurant only.

Telephone: (0795) 521404.

Conyer Quay lies at the head of Conyer Creek, 2 miles north of the A2 at Teynham, between Sittingbourne and Faversham. Well signposted.

Approx. distance of walk: 6½ miles. O.S. Map No. 178 TQ 962/648

Parking is limited to the lane beside the pub.

Although long, this level walk explores the Saxon Shore Way beside Conyer Creek and the Swale Estuary, returning along little used dead-end lanes. An excellent walk for bird lovers with the opportunity to see various waders, ducks, gulls and herons. Take your binoculars.

1. Leave the inn, turn right along the road and turn right, where road curves sharp left, onto a waymarked pitted track leading to Conyer Dock. Pass beside a Chandlery and continue across a boatyard to follow a track up onto a raised bank and path. Turn right, cross a stile and proceed on the delightful path - Saxon Shore Way - beside Conyer Creek. Cross a metal bridge by a sluice gate and remain on the raised bank, which soon curves left beside the Swale Estuary.

2. Continue for about ¾ mile alongside the estuary with good views across to the Isle of Sheppey and of the abundant birdlife. On reaching a wrecked hulk near an old con

crete sluice, bear left off the bank onto a pitted track, following it inland past a derelict house. Shortly, curve left with the track, which soon becomes metalled and shortly pass Tonge Farm on your left. Proceed to a junction and turn left along a lane, arrowed to Blacketts.

3. At the end of the lane enter Blacketts farmyard, turning right between barns and silos onto a track which curves left, then right before heading across open farmland. Remain on the track to reach the raised creekside path beside Conyer Creek, at the sluice gate. Rejoin the path and retrace steps back into Conyer and the pub.

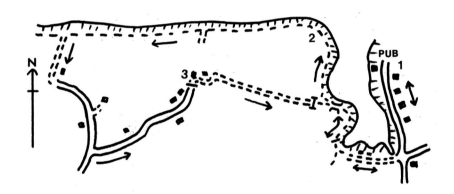

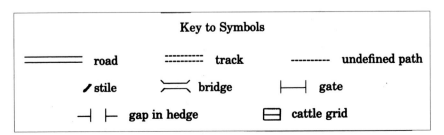

Key to Symbols

═══ road	---------- track	---------- undefined path
✔ stile	⊃—< bridge	├—┤ gate
┤ ├ gap in hedge	⊟ cattle grid	

The Dove, Dargate

Situated in the delightfully named Plum Pudding Lane beneath Blean Wood, this friendly and unpretentious honeysuckle and rose-clad brick pub was originally a thatched cottage built in 1570. It began as a home-brew house over 150 years ago and over the years has been altered and extended to the front leaving the old cottage unrecognisable to the rear. It is an idyllic summer pub with a peaceful mature garden complete with trees, dovecote, rockery and pool and masses of colourful cottage flowers. Pine abounds inside the homely rambling bar, from the floor and the wood-panelled walls to the rustic stripped and scrubbed pine tables and pews. An open fire warms the bar and old framed photographs of the pub and village in bygone days adorn the walls. A small family side room is furnished with modern pine and comfortable rush-seated ladder-backed chairs. The relaxing country atmosphere is enhanced by the lack of both piped music and the intrusion of electronic games.

The pub is owned by Shepherd Neame and well run by landlord Simon Blount who dispenses a good pint of their ever popular Master Brew all year, with the addition of Spitfire Bitter and Porter during the winter months.

A short regularly changing blackboard menu emphasises hearty home-cooked fare that is served daily, except Sunday evenings, between 12 noon and 2pm and from 7pm till 9pm. Choices may include steak and kidney pie, mixed grill, vegetable or chicken curry, nut and mushroom fettucini and a range of fresh fish dishes such as halibut steak, grilled plaice, garlic king prawns and fishermans pie. Puddings include hot chocolate fudge cake. On each table a hand-written card lists the bar snack menu which features garlic bread, a selection of sandwiches, ploughmans, filled baked potatoes, chilli, cottage pie and corned beef hash. Chips can only be found on the separate childrens menu. Barbeques in the splendid garden are a summer attraction.

Weekday opening times are from 11am till 3pm and from 6pm till 11pm.

Both children and dogs are welcome in the pub.

Telephone: (0227) 751360.

Village signposted off the A299, 4 miles west of Whitstable.

Approx. distance of walk: 3 miles. O.S. Map No. 179 TR 080/615

The inn has its own car park.

A short peaceful woodland walk through Blean Wood up to Holly Hill. Superb open views across the marshes to the Swale and the Isle of Sheppey. Gentle climbing, but the woodland paths can be very muddy and slippery after wet weather.

1. Cross the road from the pub and follow the lane signposted Herne Hill and Boughton. Where the road curves right, bear off left beside a weatherboarded cottage onto a waymarked bridleway. At a fork of paths on the woodland edge, keep left and soon enter this delightful mainly beech woodland. Remain on the established path, gently climbing uphill to emerge into a farmyard.
2. Follow the track through the farm between barns. Pass through a gate, then almost immediately turn sharp right (good views) through a further gate (blue arrow) to follow a pitted track towards a house. Keep ahead where track enters the drive of the house, pass through a metal gate and remain on the main worn pathway, fringed with rhododendrons, through woodland. Curve left, shortly to follow woodland fringe with fine views across Seasalter, Whitstable and the Isle of Sheppey. At a fork of paths, keep right to a gate and a lane.
3. Turn right down the narrow little used lane to a T-junction and turn right again. Follow the lane for $\frac{1}{4}$ mile, then bear left through a metal gate (yellow arrow) and pass The Old Gate House. Keep to the metalled farm track, bearing right at a fork and shortly reach a lane. Turn right back to the pub.

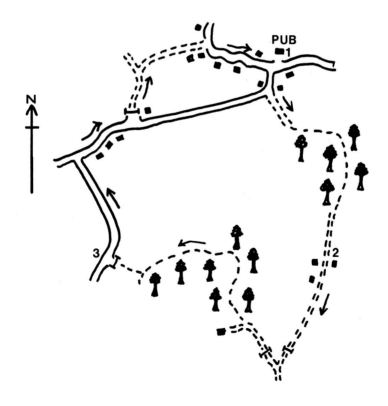

The Carpenters Arms, Eastling

Nestling on a lane in a very rural hamlet, the Carpenters dates back to 1380 when it was built as an early Kentish Hall House. It became an ale house quite early on in its history, providing refreshment for the carpenters who worked in the sawmill at the back of the magnificent manor house across the road, which was the birthplace of the noted Kentish historian Edward Hasted. The mellow brick facade belies its age hiding the ancient, part-timbered original building which teems with character. The single bar boasts a wealth of beams, a huge brick inglenook with warming log fire and a collection of old furniture, including numerous pews around draw-leaf dining room tables. Plenty of bygones, farming implements, old local photographs, stuffed birds and old bottles adorn the room, while the profusion of pot plants and the candle-topped tables enhance the relaxing, homely atmosphere. The separate, cosy low beamed restaurant features a red-brick floor, a vast inglenook with bread oven and lace clothed tables complete with fresh flowers and candles. A friendly Irish welcome is guaranteed from licensees Tony and Mary O'Regan who have successfully run this Shepherd Neame establishment for the past few years.

On draught are the well kept brewery ales, namely Master Brew, Spitfire, Original Porter and Mild.

The sensibly short bar menu features sound home-cooked favourites such as steak and kidney pie, lamb casserole, chilli, beef or chicken curry, hearty soups - broccoli and Stilton, onion with croutons - ham, egg and chips, 8oz burger, a range of toasted sandwiches, ploughmans and the Carpenters countryman, a speciality ploughmans with a pound of spicy Kent sausage. Two daily specials are available and may include a game dish - pot roast pheasant - in season. Restaurant fare ranges from fresh fish dishes to good steaks served with six vegetables. Bar and restaurant food is served daily, except Sunday evenings.

Weekday opening times are from 11am till 4pm and from 6pm till 11pm. Overnight accommodation is available in three ensuite bedrooms.

Children over 7 years are welcome in the restaurant only and dogs are allowed in if they are on a lead.

Telephone: (0795) 890234.

Village is located on a lane 3 miles south-west of the A2 at Faversham.

Approx. distance of walk: 2½ miles. O.S. Map No. 178 TQ 963/566.

The pub has its own car park and walkers can use the church car park up the lane.

A short, delightfully rural walk across farmland and through peaceful woodland. Easy going and an ideal family stroll. Eastling church is well worth a visit and the churchyard boasts a fine ancient yew tree. The splendid timbered manor house near the pub is reputed to be the second oldest building in Kent.

1. From the pub car park turn left along the village lane, pass the left turning to Newnham, then enter the field on your right (not waymarked) and follow its left-hand edge. Bear right to a stile on your left, keep left-handed, then where the path joins a grassy track to a barn, turn right and keep left of a line of trees. At the end of the trees head diagonally left across the field on a defined path towards a house. On reaching a crossroads of paths by the house, turn right through scrub and across a field to enter woodland.

2. At a crossing of tracks, turn right with blue arrow and follow the wide track through the woodland fringe to a lane. Turn right, then at the beginning of some white railings, bear off left onto a waymarked path uphill into woods. Curve right then left and bear right on a narrow ill-defined path through the trees to a stile on the woodland edge. Continue straight across an open field, then just before reaching the perimeter fence and house, turn right to a stile visible in the hedgerow. Bear right across a paddock to a stile, keep left to a further stile beside house and continue across a field and along the field edge to a waymarked gap (yellow arrow), leading between properties on a drive to a lane. Turn left back to the pub.

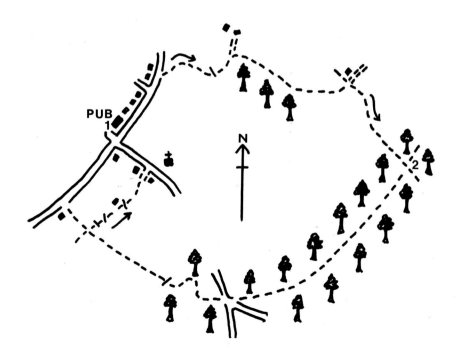

The Fordwich Arms, Fordwich

This solid Tudor-style village pub was built 63 years ago on the site of the ancient long weatherboarded hostelry that was burnt down in 1928. Enjoying a fine setting beside the River Stour, St Mary's church and the tiny half-timbered medieval town hall, it was once a crane-house collecting tolls from goods unloaded at the town quay at the time when the Stour was navigable and Fordwich was Canterbury's port. Civilised alfresco drinking can be savoured on the delightful riverside terrace and garden. The handsome woodblock-floored long bar has open fires at each end, fine arched windows and is smartly furnished with red plush seating, some in quiet secluded alcoves. China plates, various pictures and a collection of copper jugs and other bygones decorate the walls. There is also a separate dining room where children are most welcome. The pub is owned by Whitbread with the relaxing and friendly atmosphere found here being generated by landlords Nigel and Patsy Thompson.

Real ales on draught generally include Flowers Original, Fremlins Bitter, Boddingtons Bitter and Marstons Pedigree.

Good popular bar food is served daily, except Sunday evenings, from 12 noon till 2pm and 6.30pm till 10pm. The interesting snack menu includes an impressive range of 9 types of ploughmans, from local sausage to home-cooked ham, home-made soup, stuffed jacket potatoes, freshly prepared sandwiches, large filled cottage rolls and a choice of salads. Daily hot dishes are listed on a blackboard menu and may feature smoked haddock mornay, moussaka, smoked chicken and bacon in a mushroom sauce, lamb chops in redcurrant sauce, bacon and onion pudding, seafood gratin and a variety of vegetarian dishes.

Children are welcome in the separate dining room.

Telephone: (0227) 710444.

Village is signposted off the A28 at Sturry, 2 miles north-east of Canterbury.

Approx. distance of walk: 3½ miles. O.S. Map No. 179 TR 180/698

There is a small car park at the inn and some space on the village lane.

A short pleasant walk through the Stour Valley along good woodland and field paths and quiet narrow lanes. The attractive village of Fordwich was once Canterbury's River Stour port and the ancient town hall beside the pub is the smallest in the country and preserves a medieval ducking-stool.

1. From the pub follow the Stour Valley Walk sign left, passing Monks Hall and bear left onto School Lane, a narrow tarmac path between properties. Climb a stile, cross pasture to a further stile, bear left onto a track and follow Stour Valley Walk markers through the edge of a young tree plantation to a stile preceding woodland. Gently climb on a defined path through sweet chestnut coppice, then in ¼ mile lookout for a sign arrowing you right uphill to a stile on the woodland fringe.

2. Keep left-handed, passing Higham Farm (good Stour Valley views) on the left to a stile and turn right up the driveway to a lane. Cross straight over, climb a fence stile beside a gate and proceed on a grassy track to a further gate and enter woodland. At a staggered crossroads of tracks go straight on, pass beside game bird pens, then disregard the track to your left and continue to cross a small stream. Follow the track sharp right, parallel to the stream and pass through a green gate.

3. Turn immediately left along the field edge to a stile beside a gate onto a lane near Swanton Farm. Turn right and follow the lane for about 400 yards until reaching a green gate on your left. Bear off right onto a diagonal grassy path through partially cleared woodland, then descend through chestnut coppice into a field. Keep to the right-hand edge, re-enter woodland, cross a small brook and shortly reach a crossing of paths. Turn left (can be muddy) and follow the path as it bears right uphill to a lane beside Trenley Lodge. Turn left, then take the narrow lane right and descend into Fordwich. Keep straight ahead on merging with the village lane and turn right at the sharp left-hand bend back to the pub.

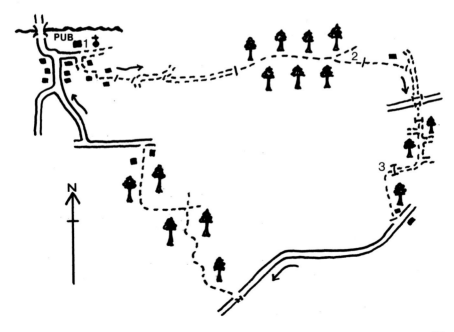

27

The Star and Eagle, Goudhurst

Dating back to the 14th century this ancient hostelry commands a lofty postion next to the parish church, 400ft above sea level with outstanding views across the Kentish Weald. Relics of vaulted stonework in some parts of the building suggest that the inn is built on the site of a medieval monastery. More recently in the 18th century it was used by the infamous 'Hawkhurst Gang', a band of smugglers who robbed and terrorised the area and it is reputed that contraband was stored in a tunnel which linked the inn to the church. Behind the magnificent timbered and gabled facade lies a vintage charm, the public areas boasting a wealth of beams, exposed brick, and a fine inglenook fireplace. Furnishings and decor are comfortable and tasteful, ranging from relaxing leatherette chairs to heavy dark oak carved furniture, including some old settles with good prints and blue and white china adorning the walls. The refectory dining room enjoys some splendid countryside views. Owned by Whitbread the Star and Eagle is one of their select inns, providing a high standard of accommodation and business facilities.

However, the character pubby bar welcomes walkers and the well stocked bar serves Flowers Original, Fremlins Bitter and Harveys Best Bitter on handpump. Michael and Karin Dimet preside over this attractive and popular establishment.

Traditional dishes are featured on the printed bar menu which lists lasagne, curry, pasta and tuna bake, ploughmans, grills, whole lemon sole, fishermans platter, chicken, ham and mushroom pie and a range of vegetarian meals. A blackboard highlights the daily specials such as tomato and tarragon or turkey and vegetable soup, roast beef and Yorkshire pudding, rabbit blanquette, poached salmon in seafood sauce and a selection of filled jacket potatoes. Sweets include spotted dick and custard, sherry trifle and chocolate fudge cake. There is a separate restaurant menu.

Weekday opening times are from 11am till 11pm.

Children are very welcome and have their own menu, but dogs are not allowed on the premises.

Accommodation comprises 11 individually styled bedrooms.

Telephone: (0580) 211512.

Village is located on the A262 between Cranbrook and the A21 north of Lamberhurst.

Approx. distance of walk: 3¼ miles. O.S. Map No. 188 TQ 724/378

The inn has some parking spaces to the front and a rear car park.

A short farmland walk through the Teise Valley, returning to the attractive hill-top village of Goudhurst via established orchard tracks. Fine rural views and an ideal walk for the whole family as the going underfoot is relatively easy. Further exploration in the area reveals Finchcocks (1½ miles west), a fine Georgian house with an outstanding collection of musical instruments dating from the 17th century. South of Goudhurst is the magnificent pinetum at Bedgebury Forest.

1. From the front of the inn turn left down the High Street into the village centre and turn right at the crossroads by the pond. Disregard the first waymarked path left and take the second arrowed route between Chequers Garage and an Estate Agents, signed Trottenden. Shortly, climb a stile (good views) and follow the worn path right to cross a stile near a pond. Continue downhill on the defined path through pasture to a further stile and plank footbridge, then keep

right on a grassy path to a stile in the field corner. At a grassy track turn right, soon to bear off right across a plank footbridge to a stile.

2. Cross a lane and a further stile and proceed straight ahead, passing between two trees to a stile and a lane. Turn right, then left beyond a pond along the driveway to Trottenden Farm. Bear right with concrete waymarker before the oast houses and follow the drive past a brick and weather

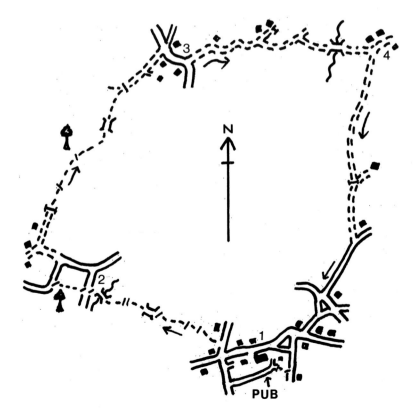

board house to a stile flanking a gate. Continue along a track, pass through a gate and maintain direction across pasture to a stile. Keep ahead to a further waymarked stile, then follow path into open pasture and bear right along the field edge to a footbridge over a brook. Keep right-handed to a stile, then gradually climb uphill on a wide pathway, then driveway to a road.

3. Turn right, then at a pink and white cottage cross over to follow a waymarked bridleway. Soon pass Swan Cottage, then just before the gates to the black and white timbered Swan Farm, bear right (yellow arrow) to join a grassy trackway along the edge of an orchard. Shortly, where the track divides, follow the arrowed route right and remain on the track across a brook, then

gradually climb uphill to Bockingfold Farm.

4. At a T-junction of tracks with the farm to your left, turn right gently uphill along an established track. Eventually, pass through a gate and keep right along a driveway to a road. Turn right, shortly to go straight over a crossroads with B-road, then keep right at the next junction to reach the A262. Bear right along the footway, then in a few yards cross over into a lane and keep left down a narrow wooded lane. Just before reaching a house on your left, take the arrowed path right up a steep bank to a stile, then proceed ahead along the field edge to a stile in the corner by a hall. Bear left along drive to a lane opposite Goudhurst church. Turn left back to the rear car park of the inn.

Peaceful parkland views at Godinton near Great Chart

The Hooden Horse, Great Chart

This unassuming, red-brick terraced village local has been transformed in the past couple of years. It is part of a small chain of pubs opened by Alex Bensley, all having the 'Hooden Horse' theme. The origins of the pub name are uncertain, but it most probably refers to the threatening prop that was used by labourers at Christmas a few hundred years ago, to collect gifts from people for the poor and needy. The rustic interior comprises a long bar with two small inter-connecting rooms. The ceiling is festooned with hops and the bare boarded and tiled floors are laid out with a simple mix of pub furniture, including wheelback chairs, stools and round tables topped with colourful candles in old wine bottles. Morris dancers are regular visitors. Generally, this tiny free house positively bustles with people, who seek out the excellent range of eight, superbly kept real ales and the interesting choice of generously served bar food that are on offer here.

Behind the well stocked bar the walls are adorned with hundreds of different beer mats, reflecting the vast number of ales that are dispensed on handpump. On my visit I had the mind-boggling choice of Hook Norton Old Hookey, Timothy Taylor Landlord, Hop Back Summer Lightning, Goachers Light, Theakstons Old Peculier, Batemans Mild, Morrells Graduate and Otter Ale to try, so it was a good job I had completed the walk first! There is also room behind the bar for Biddenden farm cider and a raft of country wines and whiskies.

Blackboard menus list the range of dishes available, for example, garlic bread with mozzarella, Hoodies bake, ploughmans platter, chilli, seafood lasagne, chicken Cashmere, pasta carbonara, chicken fajitas - chicken breast marinaded in fresh lime and coriander, served in a hot skillet with onions and peppers - vegetable burrito and nachos with melted cheese, salsa and soured cream. Puddings include banoffi pie and pecan pastry.

Weekday opening times are from 11am till 2.30pm and 6pm till 11pm.

Telephone: (0233) 625583.

Walk No. 12

Village lies just off the A28 Ashford to Tenterden road, 2 miles south-west of Ashford.

Approx. distance of walk: 4¾ miles. O.S. Map No. 189 TQ 982/421

Parking is very limited at the inn, roadside spaces being at a premium.

This scenic and varied walk through the Great Stour Valley incorporates good tracks and the well waymarked Greensand Way, which traverses both Hothfield and Godinton Parks. The going underfoot can be very wet and muddy in places after rain. Splendid North Downs views.

1. On leaving the pub turn right along the village street. Pass the parish church and a house on your right, then turn right along a concrete farm driveway and pass Court Lodge Farm. Go through the farmyard, remain on the concrete farm road with good views to the north and follow the grassy track left at its end, soon to pass in front of Goldwell Farm. Beyond the garden climb the stile on the right, pass between the house and the garage and follow metalled driveway to a lane. Keep straight on across the railway bridge and follow the lane through the hamlet of Worten.

2. Cross the River Stour, then just beyond the Southern Water fenced area, go through a field entrance and follow a narrow worn path across rough pasture and beside fencing to a stile. Climb a further stile and wooden steps up and across an embankment and track to a stile. Proceed ahead over what can be quite marshy ground in winter and cross a grassy 'bridge' between water-filled dykes. Climb a low wire fence to your right via an old tree trunk, then keep straight on through rough grass to a stile. (This course was taken because at the time of research a bridge was missing across the

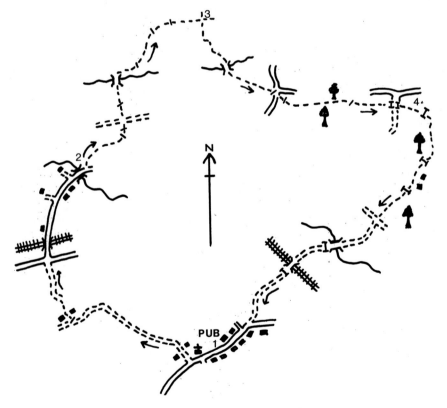

stream due to flood damage). Beyond the stile bear diagonally left across a field to a stile, then maintain direction across further field to another stile and head half-right to join a track beside some pens.
3. At a stile on your left, turn right onto a grassy path between pens and soon follow yellow arrow and Greensand Way marker half-left across parkland to a footbridge over a stream. Keep ahead beside fencing, then bear diagonally left by a dead tree to a stile in the field corner and a junction of lanes. Cross over with waymarker to a stile beside a pill box, turn left along field edge and shortly follow the path through coppice,

parallel to a lane, to a stile on the woodland fringe. Bear left through the centre of pasture and soon cross the driveway to Godinton House via two metal kissing gates.
4. Proceed ahead to another kissing gate and turn right along field edge, waymarked Great Chart. Keep right with yellow arrow along a field-edge track beside woodland, following it right again between copse to a metal kissing gate. Continue through parkland, then keep straight ahead on reaching a track, soon to cross a stream and railway before joining the lane in Great Chart. Bear right back to the pub.

Church of St. Mary the Virgin and 15th century timber framed Pest House at Great Chart

33

The Crown Inn, Groombridge

Set at the end of an attractive row of cottages, this quaint, Elizabethan tile-hung inn overlooks the village green and lies only a stones throw from the Kent/Sussex border. Originally a coaching inn, it is rumoured that it was once a smugglers haunt, with a tunnel running between Groombridge Place and the pub. The sunny front brick terrace is lined with rustic benches and is a delightful place to enjoy a fine weather drink. The interior comprises a series of three relaxing and characterful rooms. A lively local atmosphere fills the main bar which has a copper-topped serving counter, a splendid brick inglenook with log fire and original fire irons and spit and a heavily beamed ceiling adorned with pewter tankards and jugs. To the left of this bar is a small separate 'snug' room which is ideal for families. Beams and unspoilt charm are maintained in the larger dining area. Pleasant window seats enjoy the lovely village view across the green.

Owners Bill and Vivienne Rhodes offer a warm welcome to customers at this busy free house and serve well kept Courage Directors, Ruddles Best Bitter, Youngs Special and Harveys IPA on handpump. Cider drinkers can savour the local, heady farm cider from Biddenden and wine imbibers can choose by the bottle or glass from a good global list.

Tasty home-cooked food is served between 12 noon and 2pm and from 7pm till 9.30pm, except Sunday evenings. Popular bar food dishes include sound pub favourites like sausage and onion pie, steak and kidney pie, fish pie, prawn curry, ploughmans, home-baked ham and chips and local Speldhurst sausages and chips, plus good daily specials, for example, a hearty soup - leek and potato - Turkish lamb, mousaka and winter game pies. Evening restaurant fare includes half roast duck with a cherry and brandy sauce, lamb steak, halibut in oyster sauce or grilled sardines with herbs and salad. Vegetarian choices range from Chinese spring roll and vegetable curry to nut roast with Stilton sauce.

Weekday opening times are from 11am till 2.30pm (Sat. 3pm) and 6pm till 11pm.

Children are welcome in the snug bar and restaurant area, with dogs only welcome in the main bar. The inn has four character letting bedrooms.

Telephone: (0892) 864742.

34

Village straddles the Kent/Sussex border on the B2110 between Hartfield and Langton Green, 4 miles south-west of Tunbridge Wells.

Approx. distance of walk: 3 miles. O.S. Map No. 188 TQ 530/377

There is a small car park to the rear of the inn and roadside parking beside the front green.

A short peaceful walk close to the River Grom which forms the border between Kent and Sussex. The well waymarked field paths can be wet and muddy in winter so waterproof footwear is essential.

1. From the inn cross the busy B-road, pass through a wooden gate onto a fenced path between a weatherboarded cottage and chapel. Beyond a further gate follow the arrowed path across parkland towards Groombridge Place and shortly cross driveway via a gate. Proceed beside the lake, across a bridge, alongside iron fencing and beside the moated house to a gate. Keep ahead, pass through a kissing gate and join a worn path across an open field to a stile. Shortly, cross a waymarked footbridge, then follow a line of old pollarded willows, bearing left to a stile and driveway to converted oasts on your left.

2. Cross over (yellow arrow), your path soon becoming hedged as it skirts a sewage works to a stile and lane. Turn right, cross the river, pass beneath the railway bridge and shortly take the arrowed path right to a stile into pasture. Keep right-handed, pass through a gate and bear right onto a metalled driveway, following sign for Crestala. The driveway soon becomes pitted, then just beyond white cottages on your right, bear right with yellow arrow and keep left of a barn to follow path down a few steps and beside an office to a junction of paths.

3. Proceed ahead on grass centred track, cross a stream, then bear immediately right with waymarker into a field. Keep to the left-hand edge uphill, then at a fingerpost cross an open field to a bridge over a stream and continue on a worn path to a stile. Follow the line of trees through pasture to a further stile, then in a few yards turn right through a gate and pass beneath the railway to a stile. Keep straight ahead (can be muddy), then cross a stile flanking a gate on your left and continue through parkland towards Groombridge Place. Climb a stile, walk through an avenue of trees, then bear right across a stone bridge and rejoin the outward route back to the inn.

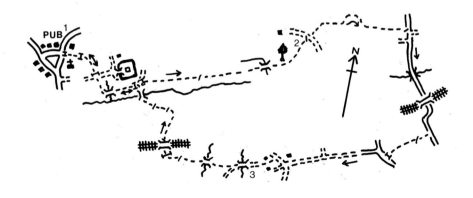

The sketch maps in this book are not necessarily to scale but have been drawn to show the maximum amount of detail.

The Artichoke Inn, Hamptons

Isolated beside a peaceful narrow lane in the depths of picturesque Kentish countryside, this charming cottage was built in 1483 and became a pub over 100 years later in 1585, as the dated cast iron fireback in the inglenook indicates. The pub remained part of the nearby Hamptons estate until the 1950's, when it was sold and it has since become a popular unspoilt rural retreat, free from the modern-day intrusions of piped music and electronic games. Tranquil summer alfresco drinking can be enjoyed on the striped awning covered front terrace or at tables and benches across the lane. Inside, two intimate and atmospheric rooms have low beamed ceilings, a splendid huge brick inglenook fireplace with open log fire, a further woodburner and an assortment of country furniture, from rustic wooden tables, settles and farmhouse chairs to wrought-iron stools and glass-topped tables. Mellow red lighting blends well with the red turkey carpet and gleaming brass and copper cooking utensils abound throughout.

The pub is a free house beautifully maintained and run by owners Terry and Barbara Simmonds. Regular real ales dispensed on handpump are Fullers London Pride, Greene King Abbot Ale, Youngs Special with the addition of the strong Youngs Winter Warmer during the winter months.

The comprehensive bar food menu is available daily from 12 noon till 2pm and from 7pm till 9.30pm. Home-made fare includes chicken and mushroom pie, steak and kidney pie, pork loin steaks marinaded in cider, garlic and herbs, chicken supreme, and a range of pasta dishes - lasagne, canelloni, pasta with tomato, onion and bacon sauce and pasta shells baked with leeks and ham. Hearty English meals like lamb casserole, and beef stew may feature on the daily specials choice. Puddings include apple crumble, tiramisu and banana and yoghurt cheesecake. Ploughmans are only available at lunchtime Monday to Friday.

Weekday opening times are from 11.30am till 2.30pm and from 6.30pm till 11pm.

The pub is closed Sunday evenings from October to Easter.

Children are welcome in the snug area of the bar, but dogs are not allowed inside.

Telephone: (0732) 810763.

The hamlet of Hamptons lies 2 miles off the A26 at Hadlow, between Maidstone and Tonbridge. From the Hadlow to Plaxtol road take the second turning right.

Approx. distance of walk 3½ miles. O.S. Map No. 188 TQ 625/523

The inn has two car parks.

A short, scenic and undulating walk through orchards, across farmland and along the Wealdway through Mereworth Woods. Good waymarked paths and the opportunity to visit Old Soar Manor (NT), a solar block of a late 13th-century knight's dwelling. (Open April to September).

1. From the inn turn right up the lane passing Egypt Farm and junction with Oxenheath Road and shortly turn right onto the waymarked path - Greensand Way - up some steps. Follow tall hedgerow, then on reaching farm track and crossroads of paths, turn left onto the wide fenced grass track and leave the Greensand Way. Proceed uphill to a lane, cross over into a further lane and bear immediately left uphill on wooded path to Gover Hill (NT). Keep left, your path soon bears right parallel with a road to reach a narrow lane.

2. Proceed straight across onto a firm stony track into Mereworth Woods. On reaching the third waymarker post at a fork of paths, keep left with yellow arrow, then shortly at a crossroads of paths turn left and proceed downhill to the woodland fringe. Bear left to a lane, turn right, then turn left into Old Soar Lane and head downhill, passing Old Soar Manor (NT).

3. Continue along the lane, across a brook, then where the lane bears right into Allen Lane, cross the stile ahead into an orchard. Turn left and follow the grassy track around the orchard edge, eventually keeping right of a farm to a lane. Turn right downhill for 200 yards and cross the waymarked stile on the left just before cottages - Greensand Way. Keep right-handed along field edge, bear right with arrow onto the track and continue on grassy track around the edge of an orchard. Bear off right at waymarked post and proceed along the left-hand edge of the field to a further post. Follow yellow arrow left on a defined path across open field and a dyke, then keep left across rough pasture and shortly enter the next field. Follow the left-hand edge, disregard the stile on your left (Greensand Way) and continue to cross a plank bridge onto a narrow fenced path that climbs gently uphill to a ladder stile opposite the pub.

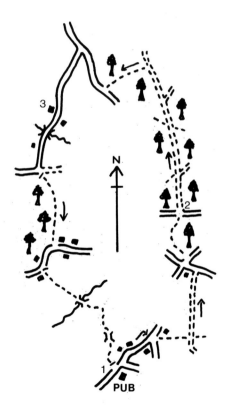

The Cock Inn, Henley Street

The Cock Inn is a 'traditional' pub in every sense of the word and a mecca for both real ale and scrumpy cider enthusiasts. Located on a country lane in a tiny hamlet, it has been a pub since the early 1700's and prior to this the building was believed to be a farmhouse. Landlord Andrew Turner has been at the helm here since 1984, but only since 1991 - when he bought the property from Allied - has he been free to develop this unassuming pub into a classic ale house and into what Camra describe as 'A shining example of how a pub should be run'.

A constantly changing selection of between 10 and 14 real ales are tapped straight from the cask behind the bar and during 1992 over 170 different brews were featured here. The countrywide choice can include Burton Ale, Youngs Special, Shepherd Neame Spitfire, Adnams Bitter, Marstons Pedigree, Greene King Abbot Ale and Theakston XB. During the summer four scrumpy ciders can be sampled - Addlestones, Sepham Farm from Kent and Bromells and Grays Farm cider from Devon.

The two unpretentious bars are welcoming, free from music and gaming machines. The simply furnished public bar has a woodburner, a bar billiards table, a few local prints and a collection of Dinky-toy cars. The comfortable lounge bar has a splendid warming log fire, wall bench seating set within the large bay window.

The traditional ambience and atmosphere of a pub in bygone days is maintained in the limited and simple, yet hearty bar snacks on offer. The choice is straightforward; either fresh bread and extra mature cheddar served with pickles, toasted cheese and onion, cheese and tomato or cheese and ham sandwiches and during the winter a bowl of hot soup with bread. In addition, at weekends during the summer a variety of barbeque dishes are available, which can be enjoyed in the rear garden and terrace. Food is served from 12 noon till 2pm and from 5pm till 8pm, (Saturdays from 12 noon till 8pm).

Weekday opening times are from 12 noon till 2.30pm and from 5pm till 11pm, (Saturdays from 12 noon till 11pm).

Dogs are welcome inside, but children are not allowed in the bars.

Telephone: (0474) 814208.

Hamlet is signposted from Sole Street, off the lane between Cobham and Meopham near Gravesend.

Approx. distance of walk: 5 miles. O.S. Map No. 177 TQ 664/672

The inn has a large car park.

An undulating and varied walk along field paths, across farmland and pasture and through peaceful woodland on wide, muddy tracks. Well waymarked, easy to follow and very scenic. Owletts (NT) at Cobham, a fine red-brick Charles II house is worth a visit (open April to September, Wednesday and Thursday only).

1. From the pub turn right along the lane, pass the Old Post Office and turn right over a stile (path 188), waymarked Luddesdown Church. Head uphill on a defined path, cross stile, pass through a narrow thicket and continue across an open field on a worn path towards the church to a lane. Cross over onto a tarmac track, signed to the church, then just before large wooden gates and barn, turn left onto an arrowed path (214) down to a stile. Keep ahead along the field edge to a stile and climb uphill between trees to an open field and a junction of paths. Turn right and follow the field edge to a lane.

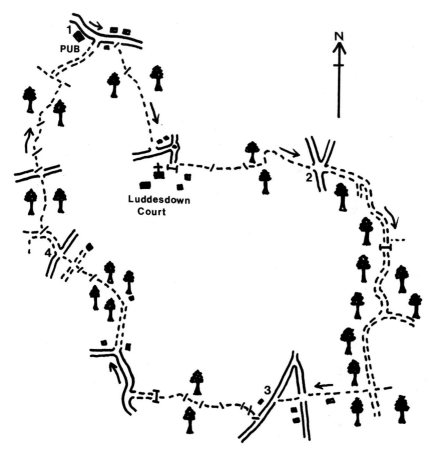

2. Cross over onto a waymarked track and continue climbing through woodland. Follow yellow arrow, remain on the main track at the top, then at an arrowed gatepost and junction of paths proceed with yellow arrow along the muddy track. At a fork, keep right, then bear left just before two pylons and follow the track through the woodland fringe to an arrowed post. Turn right onto a narrow path downhill past a cottage to a lane. Turn left, then immediately right onto the path beside 'Thatched Cottage' to a further lane.

3. Turn left, pass Great Buckland Farm and cross a stile on the right into pasture. Follow yellow waymarkers across stiles and pastures uphill to a stile preceeding woodland. Climb steeply up a stepped path to a stile, then bear slightly left across a paddock and go through a gate, shortly reaching a lane. Turn right, then where the lane bears left beside a black and white timbered cottage, continue ahead along a tarmac drive between the cottage and a barn. Tarmac soon gives way to grass, enter woodland and descend on a well waymarked path to a stile. Proceed ahead across pasture to a stile and cross a driveway onto a narrow, steep pathway to a lane.

4. Cross the lane onto a waymarked fenced bridleway, head uphill and shortly climb the stile on your right into an open field. Keep straight ahead on a worn path, descend and pass through a scrub hedge on the field edge and proceed through the next field to a lane. Cross the stile opposite, waymarked Sole Street and Henley Street, keep left-handed to a further stile, then bear half-right to a stile on the woodland edge. Pass through the wood, then follow a grassy path on the field edge to a T-junction of paths. Turn left, then immediately right onto a defined path and gently descend to the lane in Henley Street. Turn left back to pub.

Woodland track near Luddesdown

The Green Man, Hodsoll Street

This delightful white painted cottage nestles beside a small green on a dead-end lane in a tiny rural hamlet. In the summer months its facade is ablaze with an award winning floral display of colourful hanging baskets, tubs and window boxes. The name Green Man dates back to 1775-85 when it was given to the leaf-clad Mummer. He was generally a chimney sweep who walked encased in a framework of wood or wickerwork which was covered with leaves and occasionally flowers and ribbons. He would dance on May Day and other pageants at the head of the procession to clear the way. The interior comprises four neatly furnished interconnecting rooms which are warmed by a woodburner and a further open fire in the winter months. Summer invariably sees the logs in the fireplace replaced by a colourful dried flower arrangement, adding to the numerous displays, hop garlands and corn dollies that adorn much of the walls and ceilings. Floral wallpaper, old prints and a collection of horsebrasses enhance the relaxing, cottagey ambience that prevails throughout the rooms. Fine weather imbibing can be savoured in the peaceful rear garden, complete with picnic benches, aviary, pet corner and children's play area. The pub is owned by Whitbread and lovingly cared for by Richard and Jocelyn Prebble.

Real ales on draught are Marstons Pedigree, Wadworth 6X and Fremlins Bitter.

A popular attraction here is the good quality bar food that is served daily from 12 noon till 2pm and Tuesday to Saturday evenings from 7.30pm till 9.45pm. Favourites on the main menu are the range of home-cooked pies - steak and kidney, chicken, ham and mushroom, rosemary lamb, fish and seafood - as well as ploughmans, salads, filled jacket potatoes and large generously filled rolls. Daily blackboard specials may include beef stroganoff, chicken and broccoli in pepper sauce, chicken korma, liver and bacon and vegetarian lasagne. Displayed in the food counter are the choice of puddings which range from chocolate fantasie to toffee meringue.

Weekday opening times are from 11am till 2.30pm and from 6.30pm till 11pm.

Both children and dogs are welcome in the bars.

Telephone: (0732) 823575.

Walk No. 16

Hamlet and pub signposted from the A227 between Meopham and Wrotham.

Approx. distance of walk: 4 miles. O.S. Map No. 188 TO 625/630

The inn has its own car park.

A very enjoyable rural walk that undulates on well signposted paths through woods, across farmland and along short stretches of quiet country lanes. The peacefully located village of Stansted is picturesque with an interesting church.

1. Leave the pub, turn right past Hodsall House and the village hall to a T-junction. Turn left and shortly bear off right onto a waymarked by-way past Home Farmhouse. Follow the hedged track to metal gates, enter a farmyard, turn left, pass through a gate onto a track and shortly turn right with yellow arrow (footpath 254/255) onto an established hedged track. Soon follow a field edge (ignoring path right), enter woodland on path 254, then at the woodland fringe bear left onto path 204 to a stile. Cross two fields via stiles, then bear half-left to a gate and pass a pond to a lane in the hamlet of Fairseat.

2. Cross over onto waymarked path along a drive beside the chapel and Court House Farm. Proceed to a metal gate at the edge of the concrete farmyard, then beyond the fenced grassy track turn right along the field edge to a stile by a water trough across a field corner. Continue ahead downhill, cross a stile by a field entrance and proceed on a worn path to climb two stiles on the field edge. Bear slightly left uphill, follow path through woodland keeping right at the wire fence and follow yellow markers to a stile. Keep to the path, close to woodland fringe and shortly join a good grassy path. Soon bear right across the grassy valley to a stile, head diagonally right uphill to stile by a telegraph pole, and bear half-right to a stile to the right of a house.

3. Keep straight on across pasture, climb the stile on your right and follow a tree-lined path gently downhill to a stile. Continue to a stile on the woodland edge, bear right steeply downhill to a further stile and proceed half-right on a well marked path across an open field to a stile. Climb through scrub to a stile, keep left to another stile onto a path leading to a lane. Turn right downhill into Stansted, turning right at the T-junction down Plaxdale Green Road to the War Memorial.

4. Keep left, cross Malthouse Road and a waymarked stile and bear diagonally right, steeply uphill to a stile. Turn left onto a stony track, then head half-right across a large open field on a path marked by white-painted stakes to a stile and cross a lane. Maintain direction across a further field, pass through a waymarked gateway, then at an arrowed post turn left and bear diagonally right on yellow waymarked path 251. Pass through a gateway and eventually reach a lane beside the driveway to Pettings Farm. Turn right into Hodsoll Street, turning left back along the lane to the pub.

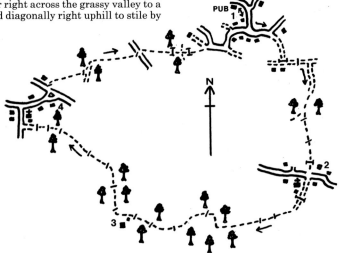

The Elephant's Head, Hook Green

This fine ancient half-timbered and half-sandstone building enjoys an isolated rural setting overlooking a green, close to Bayham Abbey and the Sussex border. Built as a farmhouse for the Abbey in 1489, it began brewing ales for the estate workers in 1768 and was known as the Elephant Ale House in 1795, acquiring its present name and full license in 1808. Inside, there is one rambling, opened-up bar - Elephant Bar - which retains much of its character and antiquity with front mullioned windows, part brick and part bare wooden floors, stone walls and a heavily beamed ceiling. One corner boasts a huge inglenook fireplace with crackling logs in its unusual raised hearth in winter. A variety of darkwood pub tables and cushioned old church pews furnish the main bar area and the cosy adjacent side rooms. French windows lead out onto a paved terrace and bench filled lawn which lookout across peaceful countryside.

It is one of the few pubs to stock the entire range of Harveys ales, namely their Best Bitter, Pale Ale, Armada Ale, XX Mild and the malty Old Ale, and are well kept by landlords Nigel and Betty Williams.

An interesting selection of home-made dishes are listed on a regularly changing blackboard menu and on my visit included lamb kebabs with rice, cottage pie, sweet and sour pork, steak and kidney pie with vegetables, tortiglioni pasta and Bolognese, mixed grill, sausage casserole in a giant Yorkshire pudding, hot roast beef sandwich, chilli and lasagne. A good vegetarian choice may include a couple of freshly prepared soups - cauliflower/vegetable - spicy beanburgers, cheesey pasta bake and mushroom stroganoff. Sandwiches and ploughmans are always available and a roast carvery is a Sunday lunchtime feature. Sunny summer days will see an outdoor barbeque, a salad bar and afternoon cream teas.

Weekday opening times are from 11am till 3pm and from 5.30pm till 11pm. During the summer the pub is open from 11am till 11pm.

Children are made very welcome and dogs are allowed in the bar, but not in the garden.

Telephone: (0892) 890279.

Walk No. 17

The pub is located beside the B2169 between Lamberhurst and Tunbridge Wells, 2 miles west of Lamberhurst.

Approx. distance of walk: 2¾ miles. O.S. Map No. 188 TQ 655/359

The pub has car parks to the side and rear, plus space to the front.

A most enjoyable short rural ramble along undulating field paths and farm tracks, close to the Kent/Sussex border. Nearby attractions include Scotney Castle (NT, open April to early November), Owl House Garden (open daily), and the 13th-century ruins of Bayham Abbey, the old church, cloisters and gatehouse being picturesquely set in the wooded Teise Valley (open daily April to September).

1. Walk along the metalled slip-road in front of the inn and turn left at the crossroads into Free Heath Lane. Follow the lane for about 200 yards and take the waymarked path left along the driveway to a pair of white cottages. Keep left of the garage, into a field and follow the left-hand edge, shortly to bear off left across a stream into a further field. Maintain course gently uphill, curve right with the field edge, and soon turn left with yellow marker across ditch into a hop field. Keep left-handed, cross a trackway and continue to a lane.

2. Climb the stile opposite, descend and cross a brook, then climb to a further stile and proceed on defined arrowed path to a stile and T-junction of paths. Turn left along narrow path beside holly hedge to a fence stile and keep left-handed across two fields via a gate to cross a track via two stiles. Continue on narrow path beside wire fence, lakes to the right, and cross two more stiles before bearing right down to a stile and footbridge. Proceed through the woodland, cross a further footbridge, then climb uphill to a stile and keep right-handed along the field edge to a stile and B-road, opposite Furnace Farm.

3. Turn left, then in a little way cross over to pass through a waymarked gate to join a concrete farm track between barns and head downhill to cross a bridge over the River Teise. Keep left along a track, then just beyond a corrugated shed turn left with waymarker into a field and follow the grassy path along the field edge. Shortly, bear off right with the path, cross a footbridge and head across pasture to a stile in front of Furnace Mill. Bear left onto the driveway and turn immediately right onto a narrow path beside the mill and enter an orchard. In the field corner bear right, then left into a hop field, keep right-handed, then on entering an open field bear slightly left on worn path and eventually reach the B-road. Turn right back to the pub.

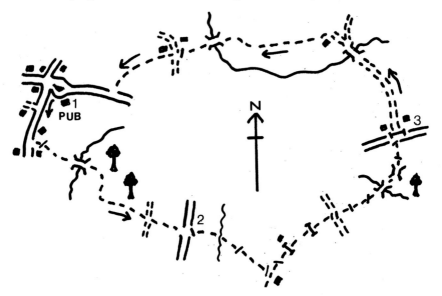

44

The Duke William Inn, Ickham

Overlooking the main street in this most peaceful and attractive village are the etched-glass windows of the Duke William, which give this 17th-century inn a 19th-century feel. Summer visitors will find the unassuming facade festooned with colourful and overflowing hanging baskets and window boxes. Originally built as an estate dwelling house it became a pub in 1804 when it was taken over by a brewer. The single cosy bar has half-pine panelled walls, a few exposed beams, a large brick fireplace with winter log fire and dotted around the walls are some caricatures of locals and collections of firearms and farming implements. Beyond the main bar is a separate comfortably furnished dining room and a splendid conservatory extension which is reserved for non-smokers and enjoys a view across the delightful well tended garden, complete with ponds. The pub is a free house that has been in the very capable hands of amiable landlords Carol and Alistair McNeil for the past 12 years.

Jocular Alistair is always at hand to help you chose from the selection of ales - Adnams Bitter, Fullers London Pride, Shepherd Neame Master Brew, Youngs Special - and from the mind-boggling list of 100 wines.

Both the bar menu and á la carte restaurant menu are extensive, with something to please all palates. Popular snacks include steak and kidney pie, mussels Provençale, large mixed salads, filled jacket potatoes, imaginatively filled banquettes - smoked turkey and redcurrant jelly or spiced ham and Dijon mustard - and a choice of pasta with at least 20 different toppings. The more expensive restaurant menu features smoked salmon, home-made pâtés and soups to start, with fresh fish and a variety of meat dishes with unusual sauces for main course. Good value are the weekly-changing 2 and 3-course table d'hôte menus and the choice of three roasts at Sunday lunchtimes - booking advisable.

Weekday opening times are from 11am till 3pm and 6pm till 11pm.

Children are most welcome, especially in the conservatory and dogs are allowed in the bar.

Telephone: (0227) 721308.

Walk No. 18

Village is signposted off the A257 at Littlebourne, 5½ miles east of Canterbury.

Approx. distance of walk: 5 miles. O.S. Map No. 179 TR 220/581

Parking spaces opposite and along the village lane.

An enjoyable gentle walk along the Little Stour Valley using a variety of pasture, woodland and farmland paths. Of interest on the walk is Howletts Zoo Park (open daily all year) and nearby is Stodmarsh National Nature Reserve, a haven for migratory and other unusual birds.

1. From the pub turn right towards the church and turn right just past Dove Cottage onto a narrow waymarked path. At an open field, turn right along the field edge, bearing left past a large shed onto a wide grass-centred track. Soon join a concrete driveway and follow it to the A257. Cross over to a stile onto path CB149, bear slightly right through pasture to another stile and continue beneath two trees to a further stile. Proceed ahead across a lawn in front of house to a metalled driveway. Bear left with waymarker over the drive and head across an open field towards the telegraph pole. Pass to its left and continue to a stile. Keep right-handed through pasture to a gate and bear left onto a metalled driveway.

2. At a sharp left bend, proceed straight ahead onto a gravel track, which soon becomes grassy, passing brick cottages to a gate. Cross a track and follow the grassy path along the base of a hill to a stile. Continue to another stile, then drop down to follow the course/channel of the Nail

Bourne (can be dry) and soon pass to the right of a fence. Proceed beside the channel to a kissing gate and a tunnel under the railway. Keep left over the river channel to a further kissing gate and bear diagonally left across pasture to a stile. Keep ahead between apple trees to a tall poplar hedge. Turn left, then shortly right through a gap in the hedge and head diagonally left between lines of apple trees to a gateway near the white Woolton Farm sign and a lane. Turn right if you wish to visit Howletts Zoo.

3. Turn left along the lane, then at a house on your left, climb the stile opposite (can be overgrown) and keep left-handed along the field edge to a stile. Proceed between wire fence and a tall hedge between orchards to a further stile. Keep ahead alongside fence and soon climb stile beside a gate on your right. Keep left, climb a further stile and soon turn left into a farm complex. Bear left beside large green sheds, then turn right between farm buildings along path arrowed

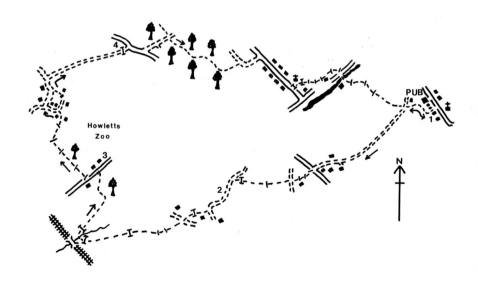

to the A257. Keep left at a thatched barn, then bear right at a fork to follow metalled driveway to the main road.

4. Turn right, cross over onto the footway and soon turn left onto a woodland track. Take the second pathway on your right and follow it through woodland to a metalled farm track. Bear right, keep right on merging with a lane and head downhill into Littlebourne. Enter the churchyard on your left, follow the path to the right of the church to a kissing gate and cross a stile to your left. Keep right-handed on a defined path and cross a series of stiles, eventually reaching a lane beside a weatherboarded mill. Walk along a grass verge, cross the road and the driveway of the mill to a stile. Keep right to a further stile, cross pasture to a footbridge, then follow worn path to another stile. Cross an open field towards a metal barn and rejoin outward route back into Ickham.

Weatherboarded Littlebourne Mill and The Little Stour river

The Plough, Ivy Hatch

This attractive 200-year-old tile-hung pub draws a discerning clientele from miles around, who seek out the outstandingly good cooking and the peaceful and genuinely unspoilt atmosphere that pervades throughout the rambling bar and smart conservatory extension. Occupying a large plot at a fork in the road in the heart of the hamlet there is plenty of room for benches on the raised gravel front terrace. The original three bars have been knocked into one large bar with several cosy room areas, yet it retains its traditional charm with part-pine panelled walls, an open brick fireplace and a collection of comfortable old furniture, including cushioned pews and benches and attractive country chairs. The modern, light and airy conservatory extension has pink linen cloths, pine and cane furniture and decorative greenery. The pub is a free house owned by Jill and Alan Ginzler and confidently managed by the chef Daniel Hamburg.

To complement the imaginative food on offer here there is a short, but well chosen list of wines, with at least seven available by the glass. Marstons Pedigree and Brakspear Bitter served on draught will not disappoint the real ale drinker.

Quality pub food is listed on twice-daily changing hand-written menus. The interesting lunchtime selection may include for starters or a light snack, a well flavoured soup - carrot and orange - crispy duck salad with spiced potatoes, braised snails and mushrooms with garlic and white wine or deep fried goat's cheese with a mango coulis. Main dishes range from spicy lamb casserole and tagliatelle Bolognese to steamed sea bass filled with red pepper mousse and steak, pommes frites. Inventive evening fare may feature chicken breast stuffed with duck liver parfait and wrapped in puff pastry, bresaola with roasted peppers and chilli salsa, venison casserole in a port sauce and pan-fried calves liver with a redcurrant and almond sauce. Delicious puddings include sticky toffee pudding, French apple flan and apricot tart. Food is served daily, except Sunday evenings.

Weekday opening times are from 12 noon till 3pm and 6pm till 11pm.

Children over 8 years are welcome in the conservatory at lunchtimes only, but no dogs inside.

Telephone: (0732) 810268.

Village is signposted left off the A227 Tonbridge to Borough Green road, 1 mile north of Shipbourne.

Approx. distance of walk: 4½ miles. O.S. Map No. 188 TQ 588/545

Parking is available at both the rear and front of the inn.

A pleasant undulating ramble along the edge of Ightham Common with far-reaching cameo views and passing through orchards, woodland and farmland on established tracks. An interesting diversion is to visit Ightham Mote (NT–open April to October), a magnificent medieval manor which the walk passes. Knole House and Park (NT–open April to October) is also nearby.

1. Leave the pub, turn right along the lane and shortly turn left at a fork into Stone Street Road. After about 200 yards turn right into Pine Tree Lane, then turn left onto a waymarked path between Beaconswood and Brackenwood properties. Gradually climb this delightful sunken sandy path along the edge of Ightham Common onto Raspit Hill. Remain on this established path (can be muddy) through trees with cameo views and eventually reach a lane.
2. Keep right, pass Seal Primary School and St Lawrence's Church, then where the lane curves right, bear off left onto an arrowed bridleway into woodland. Almost immediately turn left beside a concrete footpath marker and join a narrow path that leads diagonally left down the wooded hillside to a stile behind a house. Follow the fenced pathway to a further stile and bear left onto a driveway to a lane. Turn right and soon turn left onto an waymarked unmetalled bridleway opposite the Padwell Arms pub.
3. Remain on this wide track along the edge of an orchard, keeping left of cottages and eventually reach a lane. Cross straight over onto a waymarked metalled drive, pass a farm on the right, then at a fork of tracks proceed ahead onto an earth track through orchards (yellow markers). The track narrows to a path at the orchard edge and descends through Broadhoath Wood. Your path soon curves left and widens, passing between woodland and farmland to a lane.
4. Turn right soon to experience a fine view of Ightham Mote to your left and shortly pass the entrance to Mote Farm. Almost immediately turn left through a small gate beside the main gates to Ightham Mote and follow metalled drive right passing the splendid manor. Pass the bottom of the car park, onto a grassy trackway, then just beyond the National Trust sign, turn left through a small wooden gate, waymarked with a blue arrow. Gradually climb uphill along the left-hand edge of a field, go through a gateway and follow the defined path through woodland to a wooden gate and a junction with the main road. Turn left along a narrow path parallel with the lane and eventually merge with the lane, following it back to the pub.

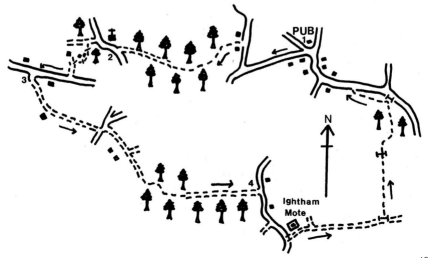

49

The Brown Trout, Lamberhurst

Set back from the road close to the entrance to Scotney Castle (NT), this pretty whitewashed cottage sports brightly coloured hanging baskets and window boxes in the summer months and is especially popular at weekends with visitors seeking out a table and the good selection of food. The pub used to be called the Rising Sun until 1980, when it acquired its present name after a nearby trout reservoir and licensees Joe and Frances Stringer have recently taken on and renamed two other pubs with the trout theme - the Tickled Trout at West Farleigh and the Rainbow Trout in Rotherfield. The bar has three interconnecting areas, all beamed, carpeted and comfortably furnished with darkwood tables and chairs and padded wall bench seating. Collections of brass, copper, country prints and encased trout festoon the walls and beams and the russet coloured hessian walls give a warm, snug feel the main bar area. Busy summer days sees seating overflowing onto the picnic-bench filled front lawn and into the large secluded rear garden, complete with a safe children's play area.

The pub is a Whitbread Wayside Inn serving Fremlins Bitter and Wadworth 6X on handpump and offering a list of at least 50 wines, including wines from the Lamberhurst Vineyard along the road.

The food deserves its good local reputation, especially the fresh fish which are delivered daily from Billingsgate, and it is advisable to book a table well in advance. Daily blackboard specials may include grilled trout in herb butter, rump steak, lasagne, deep-fried skate and chicken curry. The printed a la carte menu lists the fish choices which range from whole lobster, dressed crab and fillet of plaice to grilled halibut steak and Mediterranean prawns in garlic butter. Meat eaters can enjoy pork chops, steaks, venison casserole and roast duck, while non meat or fish eaters are well catered for. Good sandwich board selection. Food is served from 11.30am till 2.30pm and from 6pm till 10pm (from 7pm Sunday).

Weekday opening times are from 11am till 3pm and 6pm till 11pm.

Well behaved children are most welcome and dogs on leads are allowed in the bar area only.

Telephone: (0892) 890312.

The pub is located at The Down on the B2169 Frant road, just off the A21 south of Lamberhurst near the entrance to Scotney Castle.

Approx. distance of walk: 4¾ miles. O.S. Map No. 188 TQ 675/355

Limited parking beside the inn, but there is a free public car park a few yards along the lane.

A splendid gently undulating walk through the National Trust parkland of Scotney Castle - the old remains and the beautiful gardens are well worth a visit between April and early November - and along well waymarked farmland paths in the Teise Valley. Also of interest are the 13 acres of romantic gardens (open daily) belonging to Owl House, a small, timber-framed 16th-century house located a mile west of Lamberhurst. Wine lovers will appreciate a visit to the village's successful vineyard. A peaceful, scenic and easy going walk.

1. From the pub turn right along the B-road, then on reaching the A21, cross over to follow the waymarked path along the metalled driveway to Scotney Castle (NT). Pass a lake to your left and take the arrowed path right - Kilndown - to a gate. Proceed straight ahead downhill through parkland to a bridge and gate. Continue over a further bridge, go through a gate and gradually climb on defined track to a gate preceeding woodland.

2. On reaching a junction of tracks, turn left with waymarker and remain on the track uphill through woodland, ignoring turnings left and right. At the top of the rise where the track curves right, keep ahead on the pathway, shortly to pass a cottage on your left. Continue into the village of Kilndown.

Turn left along the road, disregard two arrowed paths left, then bear left along the waymarked gravel drive towards Hillside Cottage. Pass to its left, then at a fingerpost turn left up steps to a stile. Proceed straight across pasture soon to follow field edge (waymarker) to a stile in the corner. Cross a further stile, turn immediately right along the field edge to a green gate and follow a good path through woodland to a stile flanking a gate.

3. Bear slightly left on a worn path downhill across a field towards oasts to a stile and farmland, then turn left across a bridge and climb the arrowed stile on your right. Cross pasture to a stile, then bear half-left to a gate. Turn left along a grassy path below a

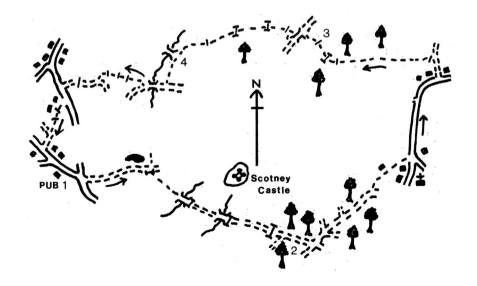

bank and proceed to a green gate, then either head straight across the open field, or follow the field edge left-handed to a way-marked stile in the hedgerow opposite. Maintain direction on the well worn path through an open field and soon follow the right-hand edge, parallel to the River Teise. 4. Keep to the field edge, disregard two footbridges right and continue to a concrete farm track. Turn right over a bridge and bear diagonally right on a worn path to a stile onto the golf course. Proceed ahead, cross two stiles, then bear left around the edge of a playing field, soon to bear left through trees to join a trackway. Turn right, and shortly cross a stile by a gate into Lamberhurst and the A21. Bear left across the busy road onto a waymarked tarmac path behind houses to a stile. Proceed uphill on a defined grassy path to a further stile, then pass through a vineyard to join a concrete drive and keep ahead to the B-road. Turn left and keep left at the road junction back to the pub.

National Trust parkland at Scotney Castle

The Bull Inn, Linton

Standing halfway up Linton Hill beside the A229, this fine part -timbered hostelry was once an old coaching inn where horses were changed and rested after the long, steep climb. The date etched on the facade records 1674 but it is believed to be much older, as the existence of a priest hole in the building seems to indicate. Like the magnificent white mansion in Linton Park, the Bull enjoys unrivalled views across the expanse of the Weald from its lawned rear garden; a delight on summer days. Being on a hill, the bar areas are on different levels; the higher restaurant area once served as the village post office until it closed in 1982 and incoporated into the inn. The wood panelled bar serves three carpeted and comfortably furnished inter-connecting rooms, all of which have part-panelled walls, beams and some exposed standing timbers. The lower, more characterful bar boasts a splendid inglenook with welcoming log fire in winter, which reflects off the horsebrasses and shiny brass plates adorning the overmantel beam.

This Whitbread house serves Harveys Sussex Bitter, Wadworth 6X and a regularly changing Mild and a strong ale, such as Morland Old Speckled Hen and has been efficiently run by David and Pam Brown for the past seven years.

During this time they have specialised in offering an excellent range of fish dishes, the fresh fish being delivered regularly from Hastings, Rye and Folkestone. Choices may include Rye Bay plaice, wing of skate, sea bass, Dover sole and cod and chips. Non fish-fanciers can order steak and kidney pie, Scotch beef steaks, roast leg of pork, lasagne, shepherds pie or from a choice of four ploughmans. Bar and restaurant meals are served daily, except Sunday evenings.

Weekday opening times are from 11.30am till 2.30pm and 6.30pm till 11pm (from 6pm Friday and Saturday).

Children are welcome in the top bar, dogs in the middle bar.

Telephone: (0622) 743612.

Walk No. 21

Village and pub are located on the A229 Maidstone to Hastings road, $3\frac{1}{2}$ miles south of Maidstone.

Approx. distance of walk: 4 miles. O.S. Map No. 188 TQ 755/502

The inn has a small rear car park and the village has a free car park adjacent to the church.

An enjoyable ramble across the greensand ridge through unspoilt parkland and orchards, affording good views across the Weald. The peaceful churchyard of the idyllically located St Andrew's Church at Boughton Monchelsea is a delight, overlooking a fine deer park and the expanse of the Weald. Easy going underfoot and an ideal walk for all the family. Boughton Monchelsea Place is open to the public at certain times.

1. From the pub, turn right along the footway and soon cross the busy A229 to follow the Greensand Way through the churchyard. Pass through a metal swing gate onto a grassy fenced path, cross the driveway to the magnificent Linton Park House - known as the Citadel of Kent with the Weald as its garden - and pass through a further gate to follow a defined path along the edge of woodland. Eventually drop down some steps and cross a lane onto the driveway to Loddington Oast, waymarked Boughton Church. Keep left, following the worn and well marked path through orchards via a stile to a gate onto a lane.

2. To visit Boughton Church, pass through the gate and turn right, otherwise follow the narrow path left and shortly cross the lane onto a waymarked woodland path beside a high stone wall. Exit the trees, follow yellow arrow slightly right across a field, pass through a gateway and cross the driveway to Boughton Monchelsea Place. Follow markers onto a grassy path between fields to a stile. Maintain direction on the worn path (good Wealden views) to a scrub area and crossing of paths. Turn right down the field edge, ignore stile on your left and continue

steeply downhill passing farm buildings on the left. Soon the path bears left into the next field and turn right along field edge to cross a stile, a plank bridge and a further stile into parkland on your right.

3. Bear half-left through pasture, pass to the left of a small reedy lake, disregard stile on your left and proceed half-right to a stile and a lane. Turn right, pass Keepers Cottage and turn left at a T-junction opposite a white house. Shortly, climb a stile beside double wooden gates on your right and walk along the right-hand edge of a field to a plank bridge and stile into coppice woodland. Follow a well waymarked path, keeping left at a T-junction of paths and shortly emerge from the wood. Head downhill to a stile and continue ahead on a wide track through an orchard to a stile by a gate onto a lane.

4. Turn left, then at the end of a wire fenced parking area, turn right onto an arrowed path through scrub to a stile. Keep straight on through Linton Park, following the line of an old fence to a stile near a lake. Proceed ahead through the park to a stile and cross the A229 onto the footway. Turn right and follow the road uphill back to the pub.

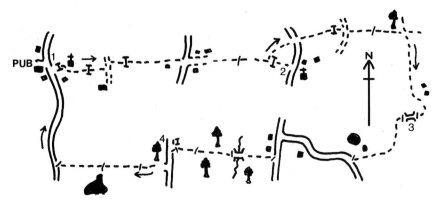

The Gate Inn, Marshside

Set beside a lane in a tiny hamlet surrounded by farmland and marshes, this splendid unspoilt country retreat is well worth seeking out. Rather than a farm gate, the pub name reputedly refers to the old gateway to the Archbishop of Canterbury's manor house at the nearby hamlet of Ford. The junction outside the pub is known as Boyden Gate. The reasons for a visit here lie behind its flower-adorned, yet unassuming facade and within the extraordinary garden. An unpretentious atmosphere fills the two charmingly rustic connecting rooms which boast quarry-tiled floors, a central brick fireplace with open fire, a delightful mix of old, sturdy scrubbed pine tables and chairs and stripped cushioned pews. Fresh flowers adorn the tables, hops hang from the ceiling beams and a variety of photographs and prints of village people and scenes in bygone days line the rough plastered walls. The traditional pub charm is enhanced with the absence of piped music, just the lively 'chatter' of locals and a selection of time-honoured pub games.

The pub is owned by Shepherd Neame and efficiently run by Christopher Smith who dispenses well conditioned Master Brew, Spitfire, Bishops Finger and Masons Dark Ale straight from the cask. A beer festival is held in August.

Summer imbibing can be enjoyed in the amazing garden, complete with duckpond, stream, and an interesting collection ducks, geese and pedigree chickens, which roam amongst the apple trees and picnic benches.

Homely bar food using fresh local produce is listed on a regularly changing blackboard menu and may feature tomato soup, bacon and mushroom torpedo, steak, salad and jacket potato, ploughmans, unusual sandwiches - including the famous black pudding filling - served with lots of pickles, burgers, spicy sausage hotpot, bean and vegetable hotpot and ratatouille flan. Free-range eggs and local vegetables are sold over the bar, as is a bag of duck food for those venturing into the garden. Bar food is served throughout opening hours.

Weekday opening times are from 11am till 2.30pm (Sat. 3pm) and 6pm till 11pm.

There is a family room and children are also welcome in the eating area of the bar. Dogs are allowed in.

Telephone: (0227) 860498.

Walk No. 22

Hamlet lies 2 miles north of the A28 at Upstreet, between Canterbury and Margate.

Approx. distance of walk: 4 miles. O.S. Map No. 179 TR 220/657

Parking is limited at the inn; spaces can be found along the lane.

A pleasant marshland walk, yet despite being quite flat the views over the surrounding countryside are extensive, taking in nearby villages and hamlets. Sarre windmill can be seen for much of the walk and with a steady wind the sails can be seen moving (open daily). Also of interest locally are the ruins of St Mary's Church at Reculver.

1. Turn right out of the inn, then in a short distance climb the waymarked stile on your left and proceed to a further stile by a dyke. Keep ahead to follow the stream and cross two more stiles before reaching a footbridge on your left. Do not cross the bridge, instead turn right across the field to cross another footbridge, then turn right and proceed to a stile and lane. Bear left and follow the narrow lane with a dyke to your left for some distance, before turning left along a waymarked bridleway (Gilling Drove). Follow this track which eventually becomes a footpath through some trees to a footbridge over a river.

2. Turn left following the Wantsum Walk, ignore two wooden bridges to your left and eventually turn left through a waymarked iron gate onto a trackway. Continue along this track following the markers and pass through an iron gate onto a road. Take the lane opposite, signposted Herne, then after a short distance take the footpath left just beyond Peggotty Cottage. Pass over a wooden footbridge and keep ahead, passing behind buildings on your left. Follow markers to cross two stiles to the right of a thatched cottage and a further stile down to a road. Turn right, then at a T-junction turn left back to the Gate Inn.

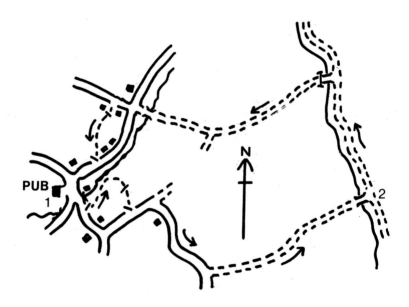

The sketch maps in this book are not necessarily to scale but have been drawn to show the maximum amount of detail.

The George Inn, Newnham

Newnham means 'new settlement', but the village in fact is very old with a Norman motte and bailey castle and some fine old buildings, including the splendid 16th-century George Inn opposite the church. Originally built in 1540 as a farm dwelling it was later split into three cottages, becoming an inn in 1718 and acquired by the local Shepherd Neame brewery in 1841. The distinctive, mellow brick and tile-hung facade hides a most delightful and lovingly cared for interior. A long wood-panelled bar runs the length of the series of character rooms which are furnished and decorated to a very high standard. Polished wooden floors are strewn with fine rugs and laid out with an interesting mix of dining tables and chairs, upholstered mahogany settles, long oak refectory tables, farmhouse chairs and stripped wooden benches. Hops adorn the ceiling and bar, while various tasteful prints, paintings, stuffed birds, polished copper, farm memorabilia and unusual collections of butterflies, clay pipes and glassware decorate the walls. Added touches include an abundance of fresh and dried flower arrangements, evening candle-light and good log burning fires, one in an enormous inglenook, which warm this most relaxing place. Sheltered garden overlooking sheep pastures.

The high standards are maintained by Simon and Ann Barnes, who also preside over the bar, serving the range of Shepherd Neame ales - Best Bitter, Spitfire, Master Brew and Original Porter - and a selection of wines by the bottle and glass.

Discerning diners come from far afield to sample the varied and imaginative home-cooked food, except Sunday evening and all day Monday. Regular menu choices include moules, chicken liver pâté, steak and kidney pie, pasta of the day, smoked chicken and basil tartlet, chilli, fillet steak with port and cream, sandwiches and a good variety of ploughmans. Excellent and more elaborate daily dishes include warm salad of duck breast with walnut oil dressing or black pudding with apples to start, followed by half shoulder of lamb with honey glaze, pan fried calves liver with bacon and onion and pot roast pheasant with wine and chestnuts. The pub can get very busy at mealtimes.

Weekday opening times are from 10.30am till 3pm and 6pm till 11pm.

Well behaved children and dogs are welcome inside.

Telephone: (0795) 890237.

Walk No. 23

Village is located on a minor road near Doddington, 3 miles south-west of the A2 near Faversham

Approx. distance of walk: 5½ miles. O.S. Map No. 178 TQ 955/576

The inn has its own car park.

A varied and easy going walk incorporating woodland, parkland and open farmland on good firm tracks and field paths. Three interesting churches can be visited on the route. The 10 acres of tranquil gardens at Doddington Place are open on certain days throughout the summer.

1. Leave the inn, turn left along the footway and take the waymarked path left beside Quince Cottage to a stile. Bear diagonally left uphill across pasture to a stile in the field corner and turn right along a metalled driveway. Pass a sawmill, keep left at a fork, pass in front of the gates to Sharsted Court and follow the track to a stile beside a gate into Sharsted Wood. Proceed ahead along a splendid woodland drive, then after about 200 yards turn right onto a wide pathway which soon curves left through the trees, eventually reaching a stile and lane beside a cottage.

2. Turn right, then at a T-junction, turn left and take the waymarked path right beside a bungalow called The Larches. Follow the field edge to the end of a fence, then bear slightly left across a field, passing waymarker post at the end of a hedge and continue on a worn path to a stile. Keep left-handed, pass through an old arrowed gateway and shortly join a track. Proceed ahead, bear left with fingerpost in front of a converted oast house and follow the metalled driveway to a quiet lane.

3. Turn right and follow the lane to a way-marked path left. Cross a field to a tree-lined hedgerow, following it behind Great Hig-

ham Farm, then continue along a line of telegraph poles and a field edge to join a worn path which soon curves right towards trees. At a crossroads of arrowed paths, turn left, cross a stile by a gate and keep left through pasture to a stile in the field corner. Turn right along the field edge, cross a stile (ignore stile right) and maintain direction through the perimeter of an orchard, bearing right beside houses onto a track to a lane.

4. Turn left, then shortly turn right onto a waymarked grassy track between Roseacre and Cherrywood bungalows. As the track bears left, proceed straight across the field to a stile, then cross pasture to a further stile and continue ahead to a lane, opposite Doddington Church. Cross over onto the driveway between the church and the Old Vicarage and keep ahead along a grassy track to a metal kissing gate and a fork of paths. Head straight across parkland towards Doddington Place, pass through a further kissing gate and continue in front of the house, soon to keep right of the driveway, downhill to a kissing gate beside the main gates. Turn left along the footway for ¼mile back into Newnham.

The Crown, Otford

This attractive white-painted, flower-decked 16th-century pub was originally a terrace of two cottages before becoming an ale house in 1860. It is picturesquely set at the top of the High Street opposite the village pond - the only area of water in England designated as a listed building - the remains of an old Archbishops of Canterbury palace and the fine restored Norman church of St Bartholomew. Inside a cosy and warm atmosphere prevails in the four inter-connecting rooms, which have a wealth of exposed beams, upright and wall timbers and two huge inglenook fireplaces. An array of chairs, stools, pew seating and tables fill the main bars, while the neat dining area has darkwood furniture with tables topped with fresh flowers and cream painted walls hung with prints and photographs. Award winning rear garden with picnic benches and pergola and narrow raised front terrace with benches. This busy establishment is owned by the Friary Meux brewery and well run by David and Yvonne Hartnoll.

Regular ales on draught are Wadworth 6X, Friary Meux Best Bitter and Ind Coope Burton Ale.

A comprehensive set of menus list the good range of bar food which is available seven days a week. Lunchtime fare includes a choice of sandwiches, filled jacket potatoes, Kentish ploughmans, Frenchmans lunch - brie, garlic sausage and pâté - beef and ale pie, chilli, fresh salads, a pasta dish and daily specials such as cod and chips and vegetable soup. In the evenings, as well as a similar snack menu, the main selection of dishes start with country pâté with Cumberland sauce or Greek style stuffed mushrooms, followed by grills, lamb kidneys 'Pascal', rack of lamb with rosemary and garlic, Oriental sautéed pork or baked halibut with fresh herbs and cream. Vegetarians are well catered for, their separate menu lists avocado and cream cheese bake and bean and nut casserole, among others. Finish off with apple and sultana sponge pudding or chocolate fudge cake.

Weekday opening times are from 11am till 2.30pm and 5.30pm till 11pm.

Children are welcome in the dining area where they have their own menu and dogs are only allowed in the bar.

Telephone: (0959) 522847.

Walk No. 24

Village is located in the Darent Valley on the A225 Sevenoaks to Dartford road and convenient to junction 5 on the M25.

Approx. distance of walk: 6 miles. O.S. Map No. 188 TQ 528/593

It is best to park in the free car park beside the village hall along the High Street.

Although quite long and challenging, this most enjoyable rural ramble explores the Darent Valley and the well waymarked farmland and woodland paths that criss-cross an unspoilt area of the North Downs. Note, there are a few strength-sapping steep climbs, rewarded by splendid country views and the going is generally good underfoot. Lullingstone Castle and Roman Villa are closeby at Eynsford.

1. From the village car park turn right - Crown lies to the left by the pond - along the High Street and soon take the arrowed Darent Valley Path right, alongside the river on a tarmac drive. Follow yellow arrow beside Little Oast to a stile, then keep left-handed through pasture parallel with river to a further stile. Maintain direction, cross farm track via two stiles, then proceed along right-hand edge of field to a stile in the corner. Continue on a narrow fenced path through a golf course to a walk-through stile and metalled track. Turn right, then at an arrowed post turn left, waymarked Shoreham and cross a cricket field before resuming route through a golf course to a lane.

2. Turn right uphill, pass beneath the railway, then at the main road take the way-marked bridleway to the right of Copt Hall opposite. Shortly, keep left at a fork of paths to follow an established path through woodland and steeply ascend scarp slope of the North Downs via wooden steps. Keep ahead at a crossing of paths, soon enter an open field and bear half-left on worn path towards barns. Join a track, bear right then left through the farm and follow fenced bridleway to a waymarked stile on your left. Climb the stile, head half-right with defined path, pass through a gateway and soon reach a stile preceeding woodland. Descend steeply to a stile and cross a golf course on a grassy path to a further stile.

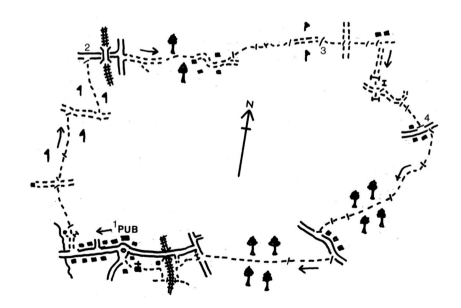

3. Climb steeply through pasture, cross a farm track via two stiles and proceed on a good path uphill to a stile close to a large house and the hamlet of Romney Street. Keep left-handed along fencing, cross another stile, then turn right along wide bridleway and pass beside a small metal gate. Take the path waymarked Eastdown, across a stile between two gates, follow muddy trackway to where it veers sharp left, then keep ahead (yellow arrow) to a stile. Proceed right-handed through pasture, climb a stile onto a narrow path and descend to a stile and lane.

4. Turn left, then in a few yards climb the stile on the right beside a gate and keep right beside fencing, soon to cross the centre of pasture on a worn path to a stile. Steeply descend through scrub and trees to a stile and follow path through woodland. Con-tinue over three more stiles to a lane, then turn left passing Paines Farm and shortly climb the arrowed stile to your right. Keep right - trig point to the left - cross a stile into woodland and begin to descend along the North Downs Way towards Otford. On reaching a road cross over, bear right along the footway, then pass through a wooden swing gate on your left to follow yellow arrows through 'Chalk Pit'. At a metalled path turn right, then shortly left along the right-hand side of a brick scout hut. Follow worn path through trees to a further tarmac path, turn right and carefully cross the railway line crossing via two stiles. Turn immediately right, then bear left beside the station car park and proceed to and through churchyard back to the A225, the village pond and the Crown.

The River Darent near Otford

Rose and Crown, Perry Wood

Historic Perry Wood hides a wealth of footpaths, the site of old Shottenden Mill, an Iron Age earthworks, the famous Pulpit - magnificent views across the Kentish countryside - and the friendly Rose and Crown pub. Dating from the 16th century, this attractive building is quietly located beside a narrow lane and is a particular favourite with families in summer for its secluded rear garden, complete with play area, barbeque and bat and trap pitch. Inside, the welcoming beamed bar is, thankfully, music and game free and boasts two huge brick fireplaces with large timber overmantels and open log fires, an assortment of pub furniture, tapestry covered stools and pew seating. Down a few steps is the snug bar which is reputedly haunted by Hammond John Smith, who was murdered at the pub in 1889, dying from twelve stab wounds he suffered following an argument about cutting and tying corn. Beyond the snug is the restaurant area which features exposed wall timbers, a grandfather clock and collections of bygones and old photographs. The pub is a free house and well run by owners Michael and Joan Jacques.

At least four real ales are stocked at one time and usually include Shepherd Neame Master Brew, Wadworth 6X, Brakspear Special, Boddingtons Bitter and a guest ale, all of which are served on handpump.

Popular home-cooked bar food is served daily The regular lunchtime menu listing vegetable stroganoff, chicken Madras, mixed grill, steak and mushroom pie, omelettes, ploughmans and a range of filled baguettes. Daily specials may include leek and potato soup, Chinese sweet and sour pork, sausage, bacon and mushroom casserole or grilled whole plaice. A few additions are featured on the separate evening menu, such as potted prawns, lamb medallions, salmon steak and a good range of steaks. Pudding choices may range from banana crème brûleé and mincemeat, orange and cointreau pie to bread and butter pudding.

Weekday opening times are from 12 noon till 2.30pm and 7pm till 11pm. The pub is closed Mondays, except bank holiday lunchtimes.

Children are very welcome in the bottom bar and have their own menu. Dogs are allowed in.

Telephone: (0227) 752214.

Perry Wood Nature Reserve can be reached by following signs to Old Wives Lees and then Selling from the A28 near Shalmsford Street, 4 miles south-west of Canterbury. Pub is signed from Selling.

Approx. distance of walk: 2 miles. O.S. Map No. 179 TR 041/552.

The inn has plenty of parking space.

An enjoyable family woodland stroll, affording good cameo views across splendid countryside. Easy going, but can be muddy in places. The nature reserve covers 150 acres and is one of the most unspoilt areas of woodland in Kent, providing a good opportunity to see a variety of woodland birds.

1. From the pub turn right onto a bridleway and soon pass close to an information board full of interesting facts about Perry Wood and its wildlife. Follow the established path around a cottage, then at a junction of paths proceed ahead with blue arrow. Keep to main path around the base and fringe of the common land with good cameo views. Curve left around the hillside, go across the crossroads of paths, then keep left at a further junction following blue arrows.

2. On reaching a post with three blue arrows, bear right onto a narrow path through coppice, downhill to a crossing of tracks, near a cottage. Continue ahead, re-enter woodland and follow arrows to a lane. Turn left and take the second waymarked path right, into the Visitors car park. Cross the

centre of the car park, negotiate some tree trunks and join the arrowed path passing between a pond and house to cross a driveway onto a lane.

3. Turn left at the fingerpost, cross the lane onto a driveway and pass through a gate. Beyond another gate keep left of a bungalow and follow the narrow path behind a large garden to a stile. Enter an old orchard with a bungalow to your left, bear diagonally left passing to right of the property and between two sheds to a stile by a telegraph pole and cross a lane onto a bridleway. Keep right through woodland (blue arrow), then right at a fork and shortly reach a crossroads of paths. Turn left and follow this path (can be muddy) to the lane opposite the pub.

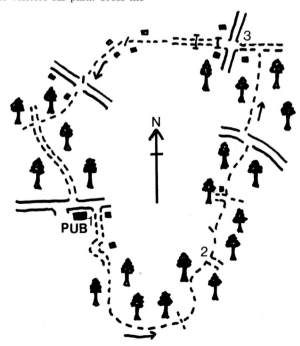

The Duck, Pett Bottom

Originally a shepherds cottage built in 1621, this attractive, long and low tile-hung building enjoys a splendid isolated position along a narrow lane with unspoilt rural valley views. It has been a pub for over 160 years and among its more recent customers was author Ian Fleming, who wrote the James Bond books and lived locally. The Duck was featured in Fleming's book 'Moonraker'. This classic country pub remains delightfully traditional in both layout and atmosphere, its two cosy bars and adjacent restaurant being thankfully music and game free. The carpeted lounge bar is warmed by an open log fire in a fine 17th-century fireplace and is neatly furnished with stripped tables, wheel-back chairs and the odd pew. Fresh flowers and candles top the tables here and in the restaurant area, enhancing the mellow, intimate dining ambience that prevails in the evening. The second bar is tiny and more rustic with tonge and groove ceiling and walls, stripped pine floorboards, open fire, a scrubbed pine table and pew and a couple of old mahogany tables and chairs. Peaceful alfresco drinking can be enjoyed in the secluded, picnic-bench filled garden to the side of the pub.

Owner Ron Brown administers proceedings behind the bar and dispenses Greene King IPA and Abbot Ale - 'Rabbits Tail' to the initiated locals - a guest beer and the deceptively strong Theobalds scrumpy cider straight from the barrel.

Hearty home-cooking draws customers to this rural retreat, the changing blackboard menu featuring such dishes as a thick country soup, farmer Browns country cheese platter, chilli, smoked Norfolk duck, filled jacket potatoes, open sandwiches, salad niçoise and mixed Whitstable seafood platter. Ever popular are landlady Mavis's pies with delicious fillings ranging from turkey and tarragon, Rye lamb and apricot to poachers, pigeon and steak and kidney. Cauliflower cheese, lasagne and a pasta bake maybe listed on the vegetarian choice and a good value 3-course lunch is available on Sundays. Puddings include spotted dick and rhubarb pie. Separate á la carte restaurant menu, except Sunday evenings.

Weekday opening times are from 11.30am till 3pm and 6.30pm till 11pm.

Children are welcome in the small back bar and dogs are allowed in.

Telephone: (0227) 830354.

Hamlet is signposted from the village of Bridge, 3 miles south-east of Canterbury.

Approx. distance of walk: 5 miles. O.S. Map No. 179 TR 161/520

The pub has a car park to the side.

A delightful gentle walk through apple orchards and along well waymarked farmland paths and tracks. Easy going with fine rural views. Nearby is Howletts Zoo set in 55 acres of parkland and home to the world's largest family of gorillas, among many other rare animals (open daily).

1. Take the waymarked path left where the car park joins the lane and gently climb into woodland. At a T-junction of paths turn left following the defined path to a stile at the woodland edge. Proceed ahead along the line of power cables, shortly to bear half-left downhill across an open field to a fingerpost and lane. Turn right, pass Little Eaton farm and take the next arrowed path right beside a tall hedge. Bear off left with yellow marker through the hedge into an orchard and keep left-handed beside another tall hedge. At a track, turn right and shortly climb the stile on your left beyond a wide trackway. Continue ahead, cross a track and walk between lines of apple trees towards a wooded chalk bank.

2. Keep left of the wood along the orchard edge, then shortly turn left onto a track beside a new plantation of apple trees. Follow the track right, ignore stile to your left remaining on the track around the orchard edge. Turn right just beyond a line of tall trees between orchards and follow the earth track left then right out of the orchard. Pass farm sheds and follow grass-centred track through open farmland, bearing left down to Lenhall Farm.

3. Pass between barns and bear right onto a metalled drive, following it to a lane. Keep left, then just before reaching a bridge and Bishopbourne sign, bear off right onto a wide trackway, (not waymarked). Shortly, turn right along a hedged grass-centred trackway. Where the track bears sharp left, continue ahead on a defined path to a fence stile and pass through a narrow stretch of woodland. Proceed ahead, shortly to follow the right-hand edge of two crop fields to a lane.

4. Turn right, soon bear left onto a signed grass-centred track and gently climb along the edge of woodland to a further lane. Turn left following the lane steeply downhill. Pass a crossroads of driveways, then pass through a waymarked gate on your right into pasture. Keep right-handed to a stile, cross a driveway onto a track and soon climb a stile beyond the entrance to Gorsley House. Follow the narrow hedged path to a further stile, pass in front of a large garage and continue ahead on a defined path along the woodland fringe. Enter the wood, then at a small post with yellow arrows, turn left retracing steps back to the pub.

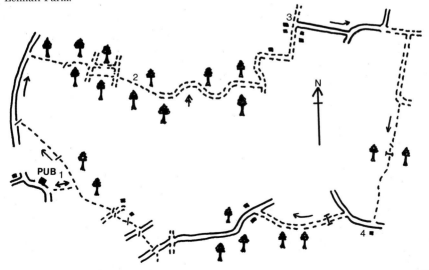

The Black Horse, Pluckley

Pluckley is reputedly the most haunted village in the country, claiming at least twelve ghosts. One such spirit resides at the Black Horse in the form of a poltergeist and is thought to be that of Jessie Brooks, killed by a ball in the skittle alley when the pub was located elsewhere in the village. The building dominates the neat village street and dates from 1470 when it was a moated farmhouse. It became a pub 150 years ago and is noted for the 19th-century 'Dering' arched windows which characterise the village and more recently as the pub featured in the TV series Darling Buds of May, which was filmed around the village. The cosy and atmospheric interior comprises of a series of inter-connecting rooms featuring exposed brick and part pine-panelled walls - some draped with old tapestries - ochre coloured beamed ceilings, some upright timbers, a vast inglenook, an impressive carved stone fireplace and an assortment of comfortable furnishings. Fine weather seating can be found in the large orchard garden with picnic benches and village views.

This friendly establishment is a Whitbread Wayside Inn dispensing Brakspear Special, Fullers London Pride, Fremlins Bitter, Wadworth 6X and Harveys Best Bitter on handpump and Biddenden scrumpy cider during summer months.

A wide-ranging menu is served daily from 12 noon till 2.30pm and 7pm till 9pm. Generously served dishes include country soup, salads, filled jacket potatoes, ham and eggs, steak and kidney pie, mixed grill, steaks, local trout, chilli, moussaka, seafood pie, chicken curry, lemon sole and a good range of sandwiches and ploughmans. Vegetarian choices include vegetable burgers and mushroom and nut fettucini. Sunday roasts.

Weekday opening times are from 11am till 11pm.

Children are welcome in the dining area and have their own menu and dogs are allowed in the bar on a lead.

Telephone: (0233) 840256.

Village is located on the Charing to Smarden road, 3 miles south-west of Charing off the A20.

Approx. distance of walk: 4½ miles. O.S. Map No. 189 TQ 926/455

Parking is available at the front of the inn.

This delightful rural stroll explores the beautiful countryside featured in the book and TV series the 'Darling Buds of May'. Orchard, field and farmland paths are well waymarked, easy going and offer fine views of both the North Downs and across the expanse of the Weald.

1. From the pub turn right, then right again at the T-junction and follow the road uphill for a short distance to pick up the way-marked Greensand Way, arrowed right across a playing field. Pass through a gap in the hedge (waymarker post), and go across a farm track onto a footpath through an orchard. Proceed ahead at a crossroads of tracks along the left-hand edge of a further orchard, passing in front of Sheerland Farm. Cross farm drive, follow markers and shortly cross a lane onto a narrow path between a wall and a garden. Climb a stile, keep left-handed through pasture, cross a path via two stiles and maintain course to a swing gate in field corner. Follow defined, waymarked path through an orchard, cross a track and stile, then turn left around the

orchard edge to a stile in the hedgerow. Bear diagonally left across an open field, keeping left of the church to cross a track and shortly drop down some steps onto a lane in Little Chart.

2. Turn left, cross the lane and join a track between Rockhurst Bungalow and Little Chart Mill. Pass through a gate, keep to the right-hand edge of a field, ignore footbridge on the right and soon bear right with green arrow onto a track to a stile beside a gate. Cross a further stile and proceed into Chart Court Farm, keeping right at a fork of tracks (yellow arrow) towards a ruined church. Soon bear off right, pass through gap in the hedge into the old churchyard and keep left to a road.

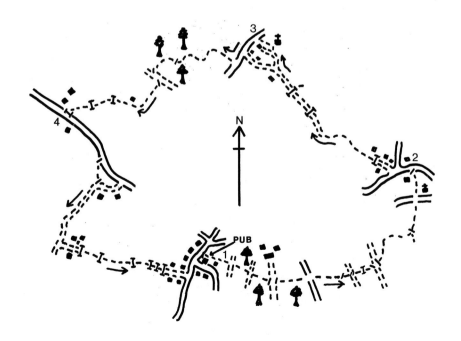

3. Turn left along the verge and shortly cross the road onto a waymarked path along the right-hand edge of an orchard. Bear left in a further orchard, then turn right onto wide track through the trees and bear left to a stile into woodland. Follow path through trees to a track, turn left, then in a few yards cross an overgrown stile on your right and head straight across an open field. Turn right with waymarker along field edge, join a grassy track and pass a derelict building to a gate. Continue to a further gate and a lane.

4. Turn left, pass Pivington Farm and in 200 yards lookout for a stile in the hedgerow on your right. Bear left up a grassybank towards cottages, cross a broken stile and turn right onto a track in front of the cottages and remain on this old established route downhill to Elvey Farm. Turn left along the driveway through the farmyard to a gate and rejoin the Greensand Way. Keep right-handed through pasture, pass through a gate and keep to the defined waymarked path uphill across fields via four gates to join a track leading to a road. Turn left, then right back into Pluckley to the pub.

Typical Kentish oast house near Pluckley

Converted oast house at Levey Farm on the Greensand Way

Ruins of St. Mary's Church beside Chart Court Farm

The Ringlestone Inn, Ringlestone

Isolated high up on top of the North Downs beside a now metalled stretch of the ancient Pilgrims Way lies this unspoilt gem of a country pub. Built in 1533, the Ringlestone was originally owned by the church and used as a hospice for travelling monks, who for many years farmed the land around it. It became one of the early 'Ale Houses' around 1615 and the original part of the inn remains much as it did then and the inscription carved in 1632 on the impressive English oak sideboard proclaiming 'A Ryghte Joyouse and welcome greetynge to ye all' is still very true to this day. Three atmospheric inter-connecting rooms radiate around the bar, all featuring brick and flint walls and floors, a wealth of oak beams, a huge inglenook fireplace with blazing winter woodburner and a delightful assortment of rustic furniture. On dark winter evenings the charming ambience is enhanced by candlelight. A later addition to the pub is the rear dining room and food servery. Attractive and peaceful summer garden with raised lawn and a rockery with waterfalls and a fountain.

Once tracked down it is hard to leave this deservedly popular free house, as it must boast one of the best stocked bars in the county. Owner Michael Millington-Buck offers up to eight constantly changing real ales from mainly independant breweries - Batemans XB, Goachers Maidstone Ale, Harveys Sussex Bitter, Adnams Broadside, Ringlestone Ale and Man O'War - all tapped straight from the cask. Both medium and strong Biddenden scrumpy ciders are available.

Excellent buffet-style bar food is served seven days a week. The lunchtime help-yourself selection may include peppered beef goulash, macaroni cheese, spicy chicken casserole and sausage, apple and onion plait, plus ploughmans, pâté, soups and a choice of nine salads. Evening fare includes their speciality home-made pies, for example beef and beer, lamb and apricot and chicken and bacon (also available lunchtimes), mussels Provençale, lamb and coconut curry, local trout and steaks. Vegetables are extra and no chips or fried foods. Puddings range from cheesecake to fruit crumble and treacle and nut tart.

Weekday opening times are from 12 noon till 3pm and 6.30pm till 11pm.

Children are welcome at anytime away from the bar.

Telephone: (0622) 859900.

Hamlet is located 1½ miles east of the B2163 Hollingbourne to Sittingbourne road. Turn right at water tower 1 mile north of Hollingbourne

Approx. distance of walk: 5½ miles. O.S. Map No. 178, 188 and 189 TQ 888/557.

There is a large car park at the inn.

A fine walk on the North Downs, across open farmland and along the North Downs/ Pilgrims Way, a scenic and established long-distance path that links Farnham in Surrey to Dover. One fairly steep climb but generally easy going underfoot. Good rural views from the North Downs escarpment. Leeds Castle, described as the "lovliest castle in the world" is only a few miles away. Built on two islands in the middle of a lake it has been beautifully restored and furnished and is set in 500 acres of landscaped parkland.

1. Climb the stile on the right beside the inn and follow the waymarked path along the right-hand hedge to the rear of the inn. Shortly, bear left across the field to a stile in the the far left-hand corner and a quiet lane. Cross the lane onto an arrowed path across farmland, keeping the hedge on your right into a field by a copse. Turn left at the end of the copse to the edge of a paddock and a stile on the left. Bear right across the field to a stile in the corner and turn right onto a track into a farmyard.

2. Pass through two metal gates, climb the stile ahead and follow the fence and hedge downhill.Cross two stiles on your left, then bear right down the field edge and remain on the defined path down to an established track - the Pilgrims Way/ North Downs Way. Turn right and remain on the track to where it becomes metalled. Turn right onto a gravel track, climb gently

uphill and soon bear off right with yellow markers, uphill through a small copse and along the left-hand edge of a field to a stile.

3. Keep to the left-hand path uphill through the edge of a beechwood to a stile, then cross a large open field on a defined path, heading between a cottage and a concrete reservoir to a lane. Cross over into a field and bear diagonally right on a path (not waymarked), and pass down the left-hand side of a copse to two stiles. Bear half-right across another field to a lane near a house.

4. Turn left, then shortly right along a lane signposted 'Camping - tents only', pass the entrance to a house on the right and proceed uphill to cross a stile on your right. Proceed across a field to a further stile, then bear diagonally left across a field to a stile in the corner next to woodland. Follow the path through a wooden gate onto a track down to the lane, opposite the inn.

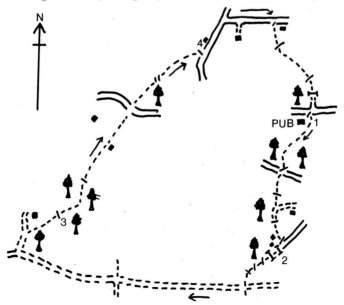

The Cliffe Tavern, St. Margarets at Cliffe

The Cliffe Tavern is a series of attractive 17th-century Kentish clapboard-and-brick buildings, located opposite the Norman church in the centre of the village. The tall, three-storey main building houses the bars and a few of the bedrooms. The front pubby bar has white painted walls with black painted timber and is simply furnished with darkwood 'pub' tables and dark green velour padded wall benches and stools. There is a small fireplace with log-effect gas fire, a few local prints and a noticeable World War II picture of an aerial dogfight adorn the walls and in general the bar has a pleasant, friendly atmosphere. The green decor extends into the rear open-plan lounge and dining room which is neatly furnished with captain's and wheel-back chairs and darkwood tables. Behind the inn is a sheltered walled lawn with rose borders and white tables and chairs. The inn is a popular free house personally and efficiently run by owners Christopher Waring-Westby and Lucie Houston-Boswall.

Regular real ales served on handpump are Tetley Bitter, Ind Coope Burton Ale and Shepherd Neame Master Brew, with a changing guest ale such as Wadworth 6X or Gales Best Bitter.

Good local produce is used in preparing the interesting bar food menus. A blackboard lists the lunchtime fare and may include cream of brocolli soup, filled rolls, ploughmans, mushroom and walnut crumble, home-made beefburgers, creamy seafood pie, beef and Guinness casserole with spinach and mashed potato, stuffed marrow and tagliatelle carbonara. The separate á la carte menu features chicken satay, green-lipped mussels, tiger prawns, Cliffe Tavern fish supper, salmon steak, chicken tikka masala, vegetable curry, roast pork in ginger and orange mustard sauce and mixed grill. Good value set dinner. Food is served daily from 12 noon till 2pm and 7pm till 9pm.

Weekday opening times are from 11.30am till 3pm and 6pm till 11pm.

Well behaved children and dogs are most welcome. Accommodation available in 12 ensuite bedrooms.

Telephone: (0304) 852749.

Village is located 1½ miles off the A258 between Dover and Deal.

Approx. distance of walk: 7 miles. O.S. Map No. 179 TR 359/448.

The inn has a car park and there is a free public car park behind the church, opposite the inn.

Although quite long, this invigorating walk encompasses the White Cliffs Country Trail which affords far-reaching views across the Channel to France on a clear day and into the busy and interesting harbour at Dover. Good well waymarked farmland paths on the return route from Dover. The Pines Garden at St Margarets and South Foreland Lighthouse (NT) can be visited and a short diversion can be made to explore the splendid castle at Dover.

1. From the tavern turn left into the High Street and proceed on the footway along Sea Street. Climb a hill, turn right with yellow arrow into St Margarets Road, then in 100 yards turn left onto a concrete track. Shortly, follow waymarkers down a long flight of steps and turn right along Foreland Road. Turn left into The Crescent, cross a track (South Foreland Valley) and ascend a chalk track, bearing right onto Lighthouse Down (NT) and the Saxon Shore Way.

2. Join the grassy cliff path with open Channel views and remain on the main defined path, which eventually rejoins the pitted chalk track. Proceed past the windmill, then just before a T-junction with a metalled lane, bear off left with waymarker towards the lighthouse. Follow the coast path sign - Langdon Cliff and Dover - to the left of the lighthouse and soon join the splendid cliff path (White Cliffs Country Trail).

3. Disregard the red arrowed path down to the beach and follow yellow waymarkers inland, skirting Langdon Hole (depression) to join a broad track. Keep left (Nature Reserve) and shortly bear off right up a railed stepped path up the cliff. Just before a wooden swing gate, bear right uphill onto a path beside a wire fence onto Langdon Cliff, beneath the Coastguard Station. Soon enter the large cliff car park, keep to the lower terrace and leave via the entrance to reach a hairpin bend.

4. Bear off left with the yellow arrow and follow path downhill to a row of cottages. Descend some steps, then bear right onto a grassy path (not waymarked) behind the cottages, parallel with the main road. Pass through scrub towards a bridge, climb some steps up an embankment to a road and turn left to cross the bridge. Take the waymarked path right, cross a stile and continue ahead parallel to the A2 through an army training ground (signs ask you to keep to the arrowed path). Follow yellow arrows along the field edge, then bear left to a gate onto a farm track. Keep left uphill through two gates and a farmyard onto the A258.

5. Turn right, follow the footway to a roundabout and taking care cross the busy A2. Pass the entrance to an MOD lane, then shortly climb a waymarked stile on your right into a field. Keep left-handed, cross an arrowed stile on the left and proceed along the right-hand edge of a field towards Bere Farm. Cross the farm driveway via stiles onto a track beside outbuildings to a metal gate. Keep left (yellow arrow) and shortly bear right-handed along the field edge to a stile, then bear diagonally right across a large open field to another stile. Follow defined path across a further field, climb a stile and walk along the left-hand edge of pasture to a stile flanking a gate. Proceed along an old track, go across a stile and turn right onto a road verge, then shortly turn right again at a T-junction back into St Margarets and the pub.

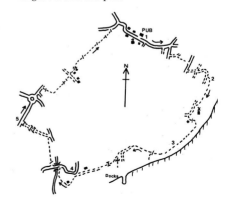

The Bell Inn, Smarden

Located beside a country lane just out of the village, this fine old tile-hung building enjoys a pleasant outlook across orchards and sheep pasture. Originally built in 1536 as a farm dwelling it acquired its ale and cider licence in 1630, but bore no name until 1769 when the sign of the 'Bell' was hung. As well as dispensing ale the building housed a blacksmith's forge; a tradition which lasted from a very early period to 1907 and during which time the hostelry offered extensive stabling and hiring facilities. The inn also supplied groceries to the local community after a grocer purchased the inn in 1878; a service that lasted nearly a century. Old-world charm abounds throughout the rambling inter-connecting bars, especially in the older, more intimate Cellar Bar and adjacent cosy room which feature low heavy beams, exposed upright timbers, inglenook fireplaces, brick and flagstone floors, old pews and a mix of candle-topped tables. The main bar is more spacious and rambles through to a lively games area, complete with darts and pool table. Ian Turner has been at the helm here since 1976, in which time he has created a highly popular inn, noted for its hearty cooking and superb range of drinks.

It is a mecca for real ale enthusiasts serving no less than 9 brews, such as Goachers Maidstone Ale, Fremlins Bitter, Flowers Original, Ringwood Old Thumper, Morland Old Speckled Hen and Fullers London Pride.

Good country fare is served daily, the changing specials list may include Kentish liver and bacon, steak, kidney and mushroom pie, goulash, fish pie, beef stroganoff, beef in beer with herb dumplings and leek and potato soup. Lighter summer dishes include Stilton quiche, lasagne and various pasta dishes. Printed menu choices range from salads, pizzas, Greek shepherds pie and pâtés to freshly-cut sandwiches and ploughmans. On sunny summer days alfresco eating can be enjoyed in the peaceful secluded garden.

Weekday opening times are from 11.30am till 2.30pm and 6pm till 11pm.

Overnight accommodation in four neat, cottagey bedrooms.

Children are welcome in the family/games room and only well behaved dogs.

Telephone: (0233) 770283.

Village is located on minor road between Pluckley and the A274 near Biddenden. Pub is situated in Bell Lane 1 mile north of the village and is well signposted.

Approx. distance of walk: 6 miles. O.S. Map No. 189 TQ 870/430

The inn has a car park and there is space along the lane.

An enjoyable easy and level Wealden walk mostly over farm and pasture land, but can be muddy underfoot after wet weather. Smarden is reputed to be one of the prettiest villages in Kent with a wealth of weatherboarded and old timber-framed cottages, including the former Cloth Hall. The 14th-century church is known as the Barn of Kent because of its width and features a 15th-century tower plus traces of wall paintings. It is well worth lingering awhile in this most delightful unspoilt village.

1. Turn right on leaving the pub and take the first lane right for Smarden, then shortly turn left along a lane signposted Pluckley and Charing. In ¼ mile climb a stile on your right before farm buildings, proceed across a field to a stile, then keep ahead over the playing field and pass through a gap in the hedge to a stile and road. Turn right, then first left and immediately take the arrowed path left to pass beside the village hall. Cross two fields via stiles, go over a footbridge across a stream and follow waymarkers across two more stiles to a lane.

2. Turn right, then immediately left over a stile into a field and follow yellow markers soon to pass through two iron gates behind farm buildings. Pass to the left of a pond, climb a stile in the far left-hand corner and follow path through woodland to a stile and open field. Cross the stile in the right-hand corner, then bear diagonally left towards farm buildings (Wissenden Farm) and cross an unmarked stile to the right of a barn into a field. Proceed ahead to an iron gate, turn right along a lane and take the footpath right just beyond Barretts Farm.

3. Cross a stile, keep right-handed along field edge to a stile, then go over a plank bridge to a further stile into a field. Turn left following markers to the end of the hedge, then proceed straight ahead across a large field to an arrowed footbridge across a

stream. Turn left, then right over a stile and keep left-handed along the field edge towards farm buildings (Tearden Farm). Cross two stiles, a gate and a further stile by a barn before reaching a lane. Turn right, follow the lane for about ½ mile to a sharp left bend, then bear right onto a farm road and pass through Hamden Farm. Cross a stile flanking a metal gate and follow waymarked track across a field to another stile and gate, then keep right-handed along field edge to a bridge and stile onto a track.

4. Continue along the track to a road and take the lane opposite, signposted Smarden. Where the lane bears left, climb the waymarked stile right and cross the field to a further stile by a gate. Proceed ahead towards farm buildings, cross a brick bridge and soon turn left behind a barn on your left to pass through a pair of iron gates into a field. Keep straight ahead to a waymarked gate, then maintain direction towards Smarden church to a stile and pass through a small housing estate to the village road. Cross over, enter the churchyard via a gate, then keep left of the church to a gate onto the lane. Keep ahead, passing the magnificent Cloth Hall on the left and remain on the lane soon to rejoin your outward route back to the inn.

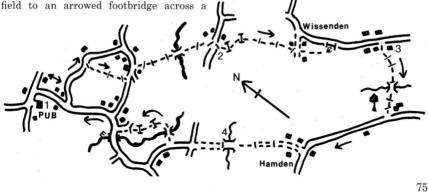

The Spotted Dog, Smart's Hill

This picturesque white painted brick and weatherboard pub dates from 1520 and is set well back from the lane, hidden by mature trees and shrubs. It is justifiably a popular summer destination as the far-reaching views from the peaceful split-level terrace and garden - some 20 miles across the Medway Valley and Penshurst village - are quite magnificent. The unusual pub name arose from a mistake during the repainting of the pub sign. It was to represent the coat of arms of the Sydney family who resided at Penshurst Place, but a short-sighted painter mistook the leopard on the family crest for a spotted hunting dog. Four blazing log fires - one a huge old inglenook - draw customers in on cold winter days, where they can relax in the charming series of inter-connecting rooms. Low ceilings, a wealth of timbering and wood panelling, quarry tiled and oak boarded floors and a delightful rustic mix of furniture characterise the snug interior. Separate restaurant area and a front function room. The inn is a free house efficiently run by Nikki and Andrew Turner.

Real ales served on handpump include Wadworth 6X, Tetley Bitter, King and Barnes Sussex Bitter, Old Spotty (a best bitter brewed for the pub by Courage) and a regularly changing guest beer and local Penshurst wines.

As well as the welcoming ambience and idyllic views, the pub is generally bustling with people seeking one of the good bar meals on offer here. Hearty snacks include a warming soup, pâtés, open sandwiches, ploughmans, salads, pies and a range of pasta and rice dishes. A more extensive choice of meals is chalked up on six blackboards, which may list Lancashire hotpot, pork steak in cider and apple sauce, lamb and fresh tarragon and red wine casserole, creamy pheasant casserole with pistachio nuts, bacon and garlic, venison sausages and navarin of lamb. Vegetarian meals may include tomato and fresh basil pie. The pudding board may feature honey and walnut pudding, lemon meringue pie and apple and apricot crumble. Food is served daily from 12 noon till 2pm and 7pm till 9.30pm.

Weekday opening times are from 11.45am till 2.30pm and 6pm till 11pm.

Children are welcome away from the bar. No dogs.

Telephone: (0892) 870253.

Hamlet and pub are situated just off the B2188 between Penshurst and Ford-combe, 5 miles north-west of Tunbridge Wells.

Approx. distance of walk: 4¾ miles. O.S. Map No. 188 TQ 522/420

The pub has a good car park across the lane.

A scenic easy going ramble through the River Medway and Eden Valleys incorporating the attractive village of Penshurst with its fine manor house. Penshurst Place built between 1340 and 1345 and enlarged in later centuries is perfectly preserved and displays extensive collections of furniture, tapestries and paintings. There is a splendid chestnut-beamed hall, a toy museum and magnificent formal gardens (open late March to early October).

1. On leaving the pub turn left along the lane, pass the old chapel and take the way-marked path left downhill beside a house to a stile. Continue downhill to a further stile and B-road, then turn left shortly to cross over onto the arrowed path along a field edge in front of cottages to an unmetalled track. Turn right and follow it into Nashes Farm.

2. Keep left (can be muddy) between barns and farmhouse and soon bear right onto a wide hedged track which ends at a field. Turn left along its edge, pass into a further field, then keep right-handed on a defined path and soon walk beside the River Medway. Bear right into another field, pass an old pillbox, then proceed across a field on a worn path to rejoin the river bank. Cross the footbridge over the river and bear left around a field edge to join a grassy track in the far left-hand corner. Turn left then with Penshurst and valley views follow it to a B-road.

3. Turn left, cross the Medway and follow the footway into Penshurst. Keep ahead at the junction in the village centre, passing the Stores and the garage, then bear right beyond the school along The Warren. Follow the metalled drive into Warren Farm, pass a barn on your left and join a grassy path to a stile. Keep right-handed along the field edge on a defined path down to a further stile, then bear half-right to cross a footbridge over the River Eden. Continue beside a fence to another stile, cross pasture on a worn path to a gate, then follow field edge to climb a stile flanking a gate onto the driveway to Salmans Farm.

4. Cross straight over, pass in front of the farmhouse on an established path, then on nearing a woodland fringe, cross the stile on your left into pasture. Proceed ahead along the field edge, cross a stile in the corner and pass through scrub to a T-junction of paths. Turn left, shortly to leave the track (yellow marker) where it curves left to follow a narrow path beside a wire fence through scrub down to a small footbridge and into a vineyard. Keep to the right-hand edge, shortly to bear right with yellow marker past a pond to two wooden footbridges.

5. Follow worn path across pasture, cross a further footbridge and proceed ahead uphill, keeping to the left of a cluster of trees and a hollow to a stile preceeding woodland. Keep to the path along the woodland fringe, shortly cross a lane and follow arrowed path up some stone steps through scrub into a field. Continue ahead on defined path towards a house and cross stile in fencing beyond the garden and bear diagonally right across two fields and stiles to an unmetalled drive. Turn right to a lane by the Bottle House Inn and turn left, then keep right at the second junction back to the pub.

The Compasses, Sole Street

Nestling in a tiny hamlet within a web of narrow lanes in unspoilt rolling countryside, this largely unspoilt white painted 500-year-old cottage has in its time been a religious premises and a carpenter's house before becoming an ale house. Beyond its flower-decked facade lies a rustic heavily beamed bar with part stone and bare-boarded floors, two huge brick fireplaces with log-effect gas fires and an assortment of simple furniture, including pine pews, tapestry covered stools and cut-away barrel seats. Hops festoon the bar, while a variety of plates, prints and brewery mirrors adorn the walls. Separate games/children's room and large L-shaped garden room with darkwood tables and chairs. Splendid lawned garden with picnic benches, play equipment, goats, sheep and aviary to keep restless youngsters amused. Lovely views across pasture.

The pub is a free house personally run by owners John and Sheila Bennet. John - a real character landlord - holds court behind the bar, dispensing well kept real ales, such as Fullers London Pride and ESB, Fremlins Bitter, Whitbread Castle Eden Ale and a constantly changing guest brew straight from the cask.   Also available are Biddenden scrumpy cider and a wide range of country wines. Good value bar food can be chosen from the extensive printed menu which lists ploughmans, assorted filled rolls and French sticks, home-made soup, chicken, mushroom and sweetcorn pie, steak and kidney pie, omelettes, chicken tikka, Dover sole, Kent hop-pickers pie, chilli, lasagne and a range of steaks. Vegetarians will not be disappointed with lentil crumble, cheese and potato pie or a cheese platter. Lemon brûlee, jam roly-poly, banoffie pie and hot chocolate sponge are among the desserts on offer. Food is served both sessions seven days a week.

Weekday opening times are from 12 noon till 3pm and 6.30pm till 11pm.

Children are most welcome in the garden room and have their own menu.

Dogs are not allowed in the bar.

Telephone: (0227) 700300.

Isolated hamlet on narrow lane off Petham to Waltham road. 3½ miles off B2068 south of Canterbury.

Approx. distance of walk: 5 miles. O.S. Map No. 189 TR095/493.

The pub has its own car park.

A peaceful, gently undulating walk along a defined by-way across the crest of the Crundale Downs, affording unspoilt countryside views and through open farmland. Easy going.

1. From the pub turn right along the lane, disregard the lane off to the left beyond Sole Cottages and proceed gently downhill to a waymarked track on your left. Follow the track between fields and shortly enter a woodland fringe on a path. At a junction of four paths turn left and follow the narrow path to a lane. Turn left uphill to Crundale church.

2. Take the waymarked by-way beside the grassy parking area, pass through a gate and proceed along a delightful path along the crest of the Crundale Downs with splendid unspoilt views across rolling downland. Beyond a metal gate, follow the earth bridleway into Towns Wood. Emerge and gently descend to a junction of tracks. Turn left uphill, the track becomes metalled as you enter hamlet of Hassell Street.

3. Pass a pink-washed house - once the Woodmans Arms - then just beyond Penang Lodge, take the arrowed path left along a grassy track into an open field. Proceed straight across, your path becomes defined and leads to a stile (yellow arrow). Keep right-handed along a fence and turn right through a gateway on reaching a woodland. Follow a grassy track to a gate and enter the wood. Shortly, turn left onto another track, then at a T-junction turn right and climb a gate into pasture.

4. Keep ahead and pass through a gate onto the driveway to Ashenfield Farm. Pass in front of the farmhouse, then keep right through a gate to follow a track between outbuildings. On entering a vast open field, continue straight ahead through the centre of the field. Cross a grassy track, maintain direction towards the field corner beside woodland to a stile. Bear half-right across pasture to a stile and turn left along a lane. Turn left at a crossroads for ¼ mile back to the pub.

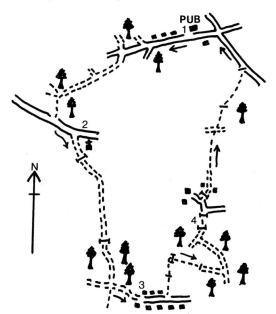

The Plough, Stalisfield Green

This magnificent building is beautifully placed high up on the North Downs, nestling beside a green in a peaceful unspoilt hamlet and enjoys far-reaching views across the Swale to the Isle of Sheppey. Originally a galleried Kentish Hall House built in the 15th-century, it was a farmhouse prior to becoming a pub in 1745. Immaculately maintained outside and in, the two beamed bars, the light and airy garden room and the cosy separate restaurant are tastefully furnished with an assortment of old and new pine tables and chairs, including high-backed settles, pews and large farmhouse fireside chairs. Candles top the tables and various watercolours, prints and old photographs line the walls, while hops and horsebrasses adorn the beams and exposed upright timbers. Two open brick fireplaces warm this most attractive country pub.

This welcoming free house is efficiently run by owner John Cole and dispenses its regular ales - Adnams Extra, Harveys Sussex Bitter, Shepherd Neame Master Brew, Tetleys Bitter and Dark Mild - on handpump. A dozen ales are featured during the mini beer festival each August.

Home-cooked food is a popular attraction here and the choice of dishes is excellent. A hearty snack menu lists thick-cut sandwiches, 5 types of ploughmans, cottage pie, ham, egg and chips, steak and kidney pie with vegetables and a warming soup. Imaginative main menu choices include dressed crab, mussels, rack of lamb with Cumberland sauce, pork Normandy and chicken breast in tomato and coriander sauce. Daily chefs specials may feature pheasant in a creamy white wine sauce, swordfish in oregano and orange, braised sirloin in shallots and red wine, monkfish in apple batter and lighter bites such as chilli and a curry. Separate vegetarian menu and Sunday roasts. Food is served from 12 noon till 2.30pm and 7pm till 9.30pm, except Sunday evening.

Children are welcome in the garden room and have their own menu. Dogs are allowed in on a lead.

Weekday opening times are from 12 noon till 3pm and 7pm till 11pm. Pub is closed all day Monday, except lunchtimes on Bank Holidays.

Telephone: (0795) 890256.

Village lies 2½ miles off the A20 Ashford to Maidstone road, signposted 1 mile north-west of Charing.

Approx. distance of walk: 6 miles. O.S. Map No. 189 TQ 954/530

The pub has its own car park.

A splendid rural walk across the backslope of the North Downs, exploring peaceful farmland and woodland paths. Excellent views south across Charing and the Stour Valley and north over the Swale to the Isle of Sheppey. Some of the field paths may be hard going, especially if ploughed.

1. From the pub cross the green and main village lane onto the narrow lane close to the village hall and follow it to a T-junction. Turn right and almost immediately climb the waymarked stile left, then keep to the left-hand fence downhill to a stile preceeding woodland. Proceed downhill on the defined path (yellow markers on trees), keep ahead at a crossing of paths and ascend to the woodland fringe. Continue straight across an open field - path marked by bags on sticks - pass through a narrow chestnut copse and bear slightly left on a worn path to join a track beside a copse to a lane, opposite Court Lodge.

2. Cross the lane, turn right through the gate into the churchyard, then bear left to a further arrowed wooden gate and follow grassy path to a stile in the corner of the churchyard. Turn left along field edge, passing silos and barns and gently descend to woodland. At a crossroads of paths on the woodland fringe, turn right with blue arrow and keep to the established waymarked path (can be muddy) to a lane. Turn right, gradually descend, then take the arrowed stile left to follow a narrow path along the edge of scrub and into trees to a stile and driveway. Turn right and remain on this pitted track to a T-junction with a metalled lane. Bear right, cross over disregarding footpath left and enter a lane called 'The Wynd'. Take the tarmac driveway right beside Mill House Lodge (splendid views left), pass through a gate and proceed to a further swing gate just beyond a converted windmill.

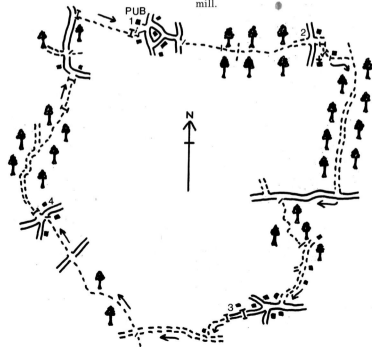

81

3. Follow yellow waymarker, pass beside a further gate and keep to the well worn path that steeply descends off the North Downs to a track - The Pilgrims/North Downs Way. Turn right along this fine hedged bridleway affording good views, then on reaching a stile on your left, bear right into an open field (yellow topped post). Head diagonally left steeply uphill, soon to follow the tree-lined edge to the field corner and marker post. Enter adjacent field, proceed across field to the edge of trees, then bear right on worn path to a lane. Cross over and maintain direction (path ill defined) to pass through wide gap in hedge in right-hand corner of the field. Cut across the corner of the next field towards a bungalow to a stile and lane.

4. Keep ahead across the road junction, climb the waymarked stile flanking a gate near the bungalow driveway and follow trackway right through mixed woodland. Shortly, bear sharp right, then left with track into a wide grassy clearing. The track soon becomes tree-lined again, but in a few yards bear off right with narrow worn path (not waymarked), uphill through woodland to a broken gate. Turn left along the field edge track, pass through a gate and turn left along a quiet lane. Ignore arrowed stile on your right opposite a track, pass brick cottages to the left and right, then at the end of a copse turn right onto a way-marked footpath through a wooden gate. Keep to this grassy path between a hedge-row and fence, eventually reaching a gate beside the pub garden. Turn left for the pub car park.

Converted windmill on top of the North Downs near Charing

The Tiger Inn, Stowting

This remote rural retreat lies in the scattered hamlet of Stowting, which nestles in some delightful countryside at the foot of the North Downs. Parts of the inn date back to the 16th century and despite changes to the interior over the years it has lost none of its character, remaining traditional and unpretentious in both atmosphere and layout. The cosy front bar has exposed brickwork and wood panelling, bare floorboards are strewn with colourful rugs and an open log fire warms either end of the room. Rustic cushioned chairs, walls pews and candle-topped tables furnish both this homely bar and the further connecting dining room to the rear. To the front of the pub a Russian vine clings to a pergola and covers the terrace area which has picnic tables and a summer barbeque. The Tiger is renowned locally for live jazz on Monday evenings. This popular free house is efficiently run by owners Alan and Linda Harris.

Four regular real ales are served on handpump, namely Tetley Bitter, Adnams Bitter, Ind Coope Burton Ale and not surprisingly Everards Tiger Best Bitter. There are generally two guest beers on offer such as Wadworth 6X and Bodd-ingtons Bitter, and for cider drinkers the excellent Biddenden farm scrumpy.

There is good choice of home-cooked bar food listed on a blackboard with a hearty soup, devilled whitebait and duck and port pâté among the range of starters. Main dishes include tandoori chicken, cock-a-leekie pie, minty leg of lamb steak, steak, kidney and mushroom pie served with vegetables, chilli, lasagne, trout and a selection of sandwiches, ploughmans and stuffed jacket potatoes. Vegetarian meals range from vegetable korma to vegetable and basil pie. Apple pie and chocolate pot feature on the pudding menu. Food is available daily between 12 noon and 2pm and from 7pm till 10pm (Sunday 9.30pm).

Weekday opening times are from 12 noon till 3pm and 7pm till 11pm. There are three double rooms available to overnight visitors.

Children are welcome away from the bar. No dogs.

Telephone: (0303) 862130.

Walk No. 34

Village signposted off the B2068, 2½ miles north of junction 11 of the M20 at Westenhanger, near Hythe.

Approx. distance of walk: 3½ miles. O.S. Map No. 189 TQ120/414.

The inn has its own car park to the rear and a few spaces at the front.

A short level walk across farmland paths and along a quiet, narrow country lane. Good scenic views along the North Downs. Fairly easy going, but some ploughed fields can make boots heavy after wet weather.

1. From the pub cross the lane and way-marked stile opposite and follow the narrow path beside a fence to a stile. Bear half-left across pasture to a stile beside a gate and turn right along a lane. Just past Chestnut Cottage, cross the arrowed stile left and bear diagonally right across pasture to a further stile. Cross a small plank bridge and another stile then turn left along the field edge (yellow marker) to a stile. Maintain left-hand course beside a tree-lined hedge and shortly bear right along a defined grassy break between fields uphill towards a church. Pass to the left of double-gates onto a lane.
2. Turn right, pass Hopton Court and cross a stile on your left and proceed ahead to a gate. Turn right along the field edge with yellow arrow to a stile in the field corner. Keep right-handed, then on reaching the gap into the adjacent field, bear diagonally left across the open field, looking out for a

plank bridge and stile in the tree-lined hedge. Continue ahead to a stile and lane.
3. Turn right, pass Smeads Farm into the hamlet of Broad Street and ignore junctions to left and right. Pass the Black Horse and shortly bear right into a field and follow the left-hand edge round to a stile. Proceed half-right to a further stile and continue ahead across pasture towards a group of trees. Pass to the left of the trees to a stile and keep ahead to another stile. Turn right around the field edge, looking out for a footbridge across a stream in the trees on your right. Cross a stile, turn left and cross another stile in field corner. Keep left-handed along the hedge, then proceed across a field to a stile into a further field and bear diagonally right on the defined path, eventually reaching a stile and lane at a junction. Head across a grassy triangle and follow the lane for Stowting back to the pub.

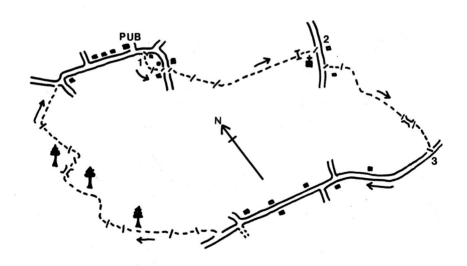

The Swan, Sutton Valence

The village of Sutton Valence is perched on top of the greensand ridge and commands superb views across the Weald. Among its tiered streets stand some interesting old houses, one of the oldest being the impressive half-weatherboarded Swan Inn, which is believed to date from the 12th century and is a typical Kentish-style building. It is possibly one of the oldest inns in the county as it acquired its license in 1467. The interior is that of an unchanged, traditional village inn with two homely bars - public and lounge. The unpretentious carpeted lounge bar has a heavily beamed ceiling, an attractive bay window with bench seats overlooking the village street, a small brick fireplace and various small stools. In 1927 a fire, which began beneath a beam in the upstairs fireplace, seriously damaged the outer wall of this bar. The unspoilt public bar boasts a huge inglenook fireplace with winter log fire, exposed black painted upright timbers and is simply furnished with stools, wall bench seating and dart board.

Whitbread own this friendly pub and licensee Tom Peters serves well kept Fremlins Bitter, Wadworth 6X and Flowers Original on handpump.

Bar food is good value, the short lunchtime menu listing a soup, home-cooked ham, eggs and chips, scampi, full salads - smoked salmon, prawn, ham, smoked trout and hot sausage - and freshly-cut sandwiches. At least two home-made hot dishes are available, such as liver and bacon, beef bourguignonne, chicken chasseur and spaghetti Bolognese. Evening fare includes pâté and prawn cocktail to start, followed by grilled Dover sole, lamb chops, rump steak, grilled gammon or the daily special. Food is served from 12.30pm till 2.30pm and 7pm till 10pm, except Sunday and Monday evenings. Fine weather alfresco eating can be enjoyed on the rear terraced lawned garden.

Weekday opening times are from 11am till 3pm and 6pm till 11pm

Well behaved children are allowed in and dogs are very welcome.

Telephone: (0622) 843212.

Walk No. 35

Village is located on a ridge, just off the A272 between Maidstone and Tenterden, 5½ miles south-west of Maidstone.

Approx. distance of walk: 5 miles. O.S. Map No. 188 TQ 813/492

Park in the village street outside the inn.

A peaceful scenic walk along the greensand escarpment with panoramic views across the Weald of Kent. Well waymarked along the Greensand Way, returning along gently undulating field paths which can be wet and muddy underfoot. Sutton Valence is a pretty village with an old ruined castle and a notable public school which dominates the village.

1. From the pub turn left, follow the raised pavement uphill out of the village and walk along the lane (Greensand Way) to a crossroads. Bear off left to a waymarked stile and head straight across an open field on a worn path, crossing a farm track before bearing slightly right to a stile and junction of lanes. Proceed ahead along the lane passing East Sutton Church and the entrance to the Open Prison to a T-junction. Climb the stile opposite, head downhill on a grassy track and pass through a gate. Ascend through pasture to a gate to the left of a cottage and turn left up a lane.

2. Shortly, turn right with Greensand Way markers beside Morry House and proceed through the top of a hop field and an orchard. Soon join an established trackway with fine views and head towards Ulcombe Church. Pass farm outbuildings, and walk along the driveway beside the churchyard to a lane and turn right downhill into Ulcombe village. Beyond The Harrow, take the waymarked path beside the school and play area into a field. Keep right-handed around the field edge to cross a plank bridge into a further field. Turn left along the field edge parallel to the brook, then just beyond some trees pass through a field entrance and pro

ceed right-handed along a hedgerow to a stile. Continue through pasture and join a track leading to a lane.

3. Cross over and bear half-left across pasture on a defined path to a fence stile and plank bridge over a stream. Head uphill beside fence to a stile and lane. Cross stile opposite, keep left-handed, then just beyond a line of trees bear diagonally left to a gate in the field corner. Head slightly left uphill to a stile and enter woodland. Pass through woodland fringe with lake to your right, cross a stile and maintain direction across pasture, over a low fence and along the field edge to a stile and lane.

4. Turn left, then shortly right (waymarked) through a gate. Proceed through a further gate, keep right uphill to a fence stile and continue to a lane. Turn right steeply uphill, pass Boyton Court Cottages and soon take the metalled drive left, opposite Boyton Court. At a fork of ways, bear slightly right onto a defined path at the base of a steep concrete road and soon pass to the side of a gate onto a metalled lane. Proceed ahead, pass Sutton Place and keep left at a fork to follow the lane past Sutton Valence Castle back into the village to the pub.

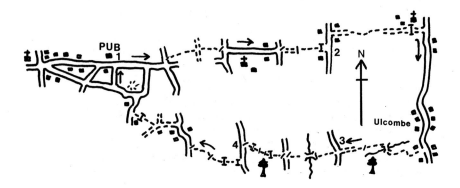

The Fox and Hounds, Toy's Hill

In recent years the demise of the 'traditional' country pub has been marked, either through lack of trade in rural areas, soaring rents or due to big brewery pressures to upgrade, extend and transform village locals into large eating houses. Thankfully, the isolated and homely Fox and Hounds, set 800ft up on the greensand ridge - the highest pub in Kent - amid 200 acres of National Trust woodland, has escaped such a fate - but only just! Back in 1986 the then owners Friary Meux tried to 'upgrade' the pub. A fierce campaign involving passionate regulars, ramblers, the local press and letters of support from around the world successfully halted the brewers intentions. Greene King now own this much loved, rustic rural retreat and have vowed not to spoil the timeless atmosphere that pervades through the two interconnecting rooms, which are divided by a central brick fireplace with log fire. A welcoming, much-lived-in and relaxing ambience exists with a rug-strewn floor, a motley assortment of furniture, including old sofas and relaxing easy chairs with throw-over covers and a selection of magazines - Country Life, Private Eye, Hello - top most of the tables. Photographs of locals and the devastation of the surrounding woodland after the 1987 hurricane adorn the walls. Fine weather drinking can be enjoyed in the peaceful, shrub filled garden. The Pelling family have been at the pub for 26 years and thanks to Greene King will hopefully be warmly welcoming customers for many years to come.

IPA and Abbot Ale are served on handpump.

Bar food is limited to a good choice of freshly filled rolls, ploughmans and a daily hot dish, such as cauliflower cheese, pastie or a filled baked potato. There is also a veritable 'tuck shop' of chocolate bars for energetic walkers. Snacks are served at lunchtimes only from 12 noon till 2pm.

Weekday opening times are from 12 noon till 2.30pm and 6pm till 11pm.

Children are very welcome as are well behaved dogs.

Telephone: (0732) 750328.

Walk No. 36

The hamlet lies high up on the wooded greensand ridge between the A25 at Brasted (signposted) and the B2042 near Four Elms, 5 miles west of Sevenoaks.

Approx. distance of walk: 4 miles. O.S. Map No. 188 TQ 471/520

Parking is limited at the pub, it is best to park in the large National Trust car park (free) which is located a few hundred yards south along the lane.

A most delightful undulating walk across the greensand ridge incorporating National Trust woodland paths, the Greensand Way and a peaceful lane. Glorious far-reaching views and the opportunity to visit Chartwell, once the home of Sir Winston Churchill. Also worth a visit nearby are Emmetts Garden (NT) and Quebec House (NT) and Squerryes Court, both located in the attractive village of Wester-ham.

1. From the NT car park locate the information board in the left-hand corner, disregard the Greensand Way path and take the footpath marked by a red, green and orange painted post. At T-junction of paths keep left passing memorial stone and the old site of Weardale Manor and remain on the main path, eventually bearing off right downhill with the red marked footpath. At a crossing of paths proceed straight ahead, leaving the red route, downhill to a stile on the woodland fringe. Keep left-handed alongside a fence to a further stile and soon join a track in front of old oasts and cottage (Outridge Farm).

2. In a little way bear off left to a stile, waymarked French Street, then descend through pasture on a worn path to cross a double stile and footbridge in the valley bottom. Keep left to a stile, then climb steeply to a further stile and lane in the hamlet of French Street. Turn left, then right along the driveway to a house called Mannings Wood, joining the Greensand Way. Proceed along the hedged trackway beside the property, then on reaching a metalled drive turn immediately left with GW marker. Continue through woodland

(good views), eventually reaching a lane.

3. Cross over and remain on the narrow Greensand Way path, downhill with Chartwell soon visible to your left to reach a stile and lane. Go straight across, climb uphill, then at GW marker post bear off left to follow permitted rhododendron fringed path beyond a wooden barrier. Splendid views across Chartwell to the Weald beyond. Pass beside a further barrier, keep left at a T-junction of paths and turn right along the lane, passing Chartwell Cottage. Shortly, turn left along the driveway to Chartwell Farm, signposted Puddledock.

4. Pass to the left of the farmhouse and beside some oasts to a kissing gate, then keep right along a concrete farm track, soon to cross a stile beside a wooden gate. Proceed on this delightful path to a stile and lane. Turn left and remain on this peaceful lane which climbs steeply into the hamlet of Toy's Hill, affording fine views. Just before reaching a T-junction, take the arrowed path left beyond the telephone box and gradually ascend into the National Trust woodland. Keep right, pass beside a wooden barrier, then at a crossing of paths turn right with GW marker and follow the defined path back to the main car park.

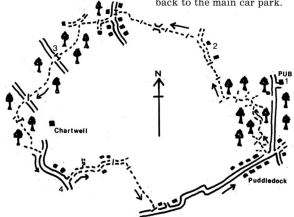

88

The White Rock Inn, Under River

The village of Under River dates back to the Magna Carta and its unusual name derives from the Anglo-Saxon word 'rither', meaning hill or escarpment. Over the years this changed to 'river', thus the name literally means 'under the hill'. Tucked in the heart of the village is the White Rock Inn, a neat red brick building dating from 1820 with a single-storey, white clapboard extension. The original building houses the cosy small saloon bar which features brick and stone walls, beams, a woodblock floor, padded wall bench seating and darkwood tables and chairs. Adjoining this bar is the attractive restaurant with lace-clothed tables and fresh flowers. The much larger and livelier public bar fills the weatherboard extension and contains the dart board, pool and bar billiards table. More traditional pub games can be played, namely chess, cribbage, draughts and shove ha'penny and located in the garden is a Bat and Trap pitch. The well tended lawned garden enjoys rural views and is a popular summer attraction, especially when the barbecue has been lit.

The landlord of this friendly free house is keen on offering a range of real ales. The selection may include Fullers ESB, Harveys Sussex Bitter, Marstons Pedigree, Websters Yorkshire Bitter and generally two guest beers.

An interesting choice of bar meals are chalked up on a large blackboard menu and served daily from 12 noon till 2pm and 7pm till 9.30pm (Sunday 9pm). Favourite bar snacks include generously filled baps, ploughmans and basket meals. Regular and weekly-changing dishes include pea and ham soup, giant filled Yorkshire puddings, smoked hake en-croute, chargrilled pork de Provence, supreme of chicken in a Stilton sauce, steaks and macaroni cheese. Vegetarians are well catered for with vegetable curry, tagliatelle with brocolli, mushrooms and cheese and vegetable lasagne. Walking appetites can be satisfied with spotted dick, treacle pudding or apple and sultana sponge for pudding. Traditional Sunday roasts.

Weekday opening times are from 12 noon till 3.30pm and 6pm till 11pm.

Children are most welcome in the public bar and restaurant. No dogs.

Telephone: (0732) 833112.

Walk No. 37

Village signposted off the B245 between Sevenoaks and Hildenborough.

Approx. distance of walk: 4 miles. O.S. Map No. 188 TQ 557/521

Walkers are welcome to park in the large rear car park.

A delightful walk exploring the Greensand Way along the high wooded and scenic ridge overlooking Tonbridge and the western edge of the Weald. Unrivalled views, well waymarked paths (some can be muddy) and close to the splendid National Trust properties of Knole Park and Ightham Mote (both open April-October).

1. From the inn turn right along the lane and take the arrowed bridleway beside Valley Farm. Pass in front of a house named Black Charles - a listed historic building of Kent - and begin to climb steadily uphill on a splendid old routeway. Just before a farm lane, turn right onto a path between renovated oasts and a house and continue the climb to the top of the ridge, on what can be a muddy, sunken path. Climb the stile on your right and follow narrow fenced path (Greensand Way), with magnificent views, to a lane.

2. Cross straight over onto a waymarked track, then at a fork of tracks keep left gently uphill, passing White Rock Farm on your right. Continue along a signed path which gently undulates through scrub and woodland - abundant birdlife - along the crest of the ridge. On reaching a lane turn left steeply uphill for a short distance and take the arrowed path right through the woodland fringe. Soon cross a stile into National Trust land of Ightham Mote and follow the narrow path to a further stile onto a track by a cottage.

3. Cross the waymarked stile on your right and proceed downhill across pasture to a further stile. Keep right-handed along the field-edge path, downhill across a small footbridge and follow the worn path slightly right to a stile beside a gate onto a lane. Turn right, then right again onto the driveway to Great Budds (waymarked). Keep right to stile flanking a gate, pass a pond, cross a further stile and continue on a track and later a defined path across an open field to two stiles. Maintain direction through pasture to a stile and cross a farmyard to a gate. Keep right along the edge of woodland towards Under River House and cross a stile in the field corner. Follow the path right, then bear left between tall fir trees to the driveway and turn right, soon to reach a lane. Bear right, shortly climb an arrowed stile left and head straight across pasture to a stile. Turn half-left with arrow and soon pick up a defined east-west grassy path to a stile. Continue across two stiles, then keep left-handed alongside trees to a stile and lane in Under River. Turn left back to the pub.

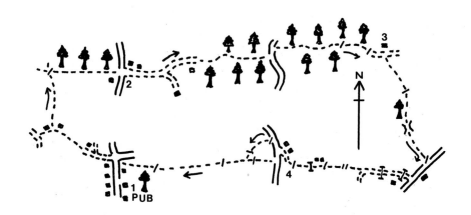

The Harrow, Warren Street

Situated high up on the North Downs in an isolated rural hamlet, this large, part weatherboarded old inn was once the forge and rest house for travellers to Canterbury along the ancient Pilgrims Way. In recent years the inn has been comfortably refurbished and extended from its low beamed 17th-century core, offering a relaxing atmosphere and spacious, well appointed accommodation. The one, very neat carpeted bar is furnished with simple cushioned chairs and round tables topped with candles and fresh flowers, and is warmed by a winter woodburner in an inglenook fireplace. Various prints and horsebrasses decorate the walls. Both the bar and the separate attractive restaurant have their own patios for peaceful, summer alfresco dining and there is also a secluded and tidy bench-filled garden.

The Harrow is a free house and is lovingly maintained by resident owners Sheila Burns and Alan Cole. Real ales served on draught include the regular local brew Shepherd Neame Master Brew Bitter and two guest beers, such as Ruddles County and Goachers Bitter.

Reliably good bar food ranges from firm pub favourites - omelettes, steaks, ploughmans, sandwiches, salads and jacket potatoes - to more imaginative choices, such as salmon en croûte, oven-baked plaice, chicken fricasée and steak and mushroom pie, all served with fresh vegetables. Spintons restaurant fare is more elaborate with Stilton filo parcels, fan of avocado with blueberry coulis or ravioli du carnard to begin your meal, followed by trellis of salmon and cod, pigeon framboise, braised guinea fowl, roast breast of duck filled with apples, sultanas and cinnamom, served with a Calvados sauce and rack of lamb filled with a spinach and chicken mousse, to name but a few. Tempting puddings include walnut pie, bread and butter pudding and lemon cheesecake. Vegetarian choices and traditional Sunday lunches. Food is served daily from 12 noon till 2pm and 7pm till 10pm.

Weekday opening times are from 11.30am till 2.30pm and 7pm till 11pm. Overnight accommodation in 15 ensuite bedrooms.

Children are welcome away from the bar, but dogs are not allowed in.

Telephone: (0622) 858727.

Walk No. 38

Hamlet is located on top of the North Downs, 1 mile north of the A20 between Maidstone and Charing, just east of Lenham.

Approx. distance of walk: 4½ miles. O.S. Map No. 189 TQ 927/529

The pub has a good large car park.

An enjoyable rural walk through farmland on the backslope of the North Downs, returning along the long-distance path - the North Downs Way/Pilgrims Way - a scenic and peaceful trackway that traverses the scarp slope of the Downs. At certain times of the year heavily ploughed fields can make the going difficult underfoot.

1. Leave the inn, turn left along the lane, then where the road curves left bear off right at the footpath fingerpost into a large open field. Head diagonally left, then on reaching a trackway follow it right and keep ahead where it ends across a field to a stile preceeding woodland. Pass through the wood and proceed straight on across the centre of a large field, between telegraph poles to a stile and lane, opposite Bleak Cottage.

2. Turn left, pass pub, cross the lane and turn right along a track, passing The Bungalow and Pond Cottage. Pass a garage, go through a gate and shortly follow the waymarked path across the front of Woodside Green Cottage to a stile and junction of paths. Turn left along the field edge and beside a garden fence to a lane. Turn left, pass High Farm, then at a T-junction proceed straight across onto a waymarked path into an open field. Bear half-left towards a building just visible in the trees and climb two stiles (can be overgrown) onto a driveway. Bear right, then left across a stile, or through the gap in the fence and descend diagonally left across a field (good views) to a gate in the far corner.

3. Turn left onto the North Downs Way, keep ahead along the lane and soon bear off left onto a metalled lane, beyond a row of cottages. Shortly pass through a gate onto a grassy track, following the North Downs Way beneath the war memorial cross etched in the chalk hillside to a gate. Continue on the hedged path to a lane and turn left uphill. Disregard the first arrowed path right, take the second waymarked path (NDW) and remain on this path to a narrow lane. Turn left steeply uphill, eventually turning left at a T-junction back to the inn.

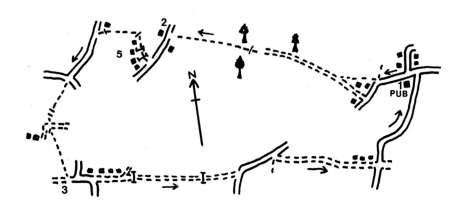

The sketch maps in this book are not necessarily to scale but have been drawn to show the maximum amount of detail.

The Endeavour, Wootton

Peacefully located in a rural village, this rustic 600-year-old brick building nestles beneath an old, clay-tiled roof and was at one time two cottages. It is reputed to be haunted by a monk called Matthew, who was hung at neaby Oak Island - just past the church - and whose body was stored in the cellar. The impression locally is that he roams the village, haunting many of the houses. The unpretentious, traditional atmosphere is maintained in the three, carpeted inter-connecting rooms, which are free from the intrusion of both music and electronic games. The main bar has a large, solid central fireplace with warming woodburner, which separates the small games area - darts, bar billiards -from the seating area. Floral curtains, cushioned stools, padded pine pews and an assortment of rustic wooden furniture characterise the simply adorned rooms. Quiet, fine weather drinking can be enjoyed in the front bench-filled garden. Popular events here are the regular quiz nights and the conker competition held every October. Owner Sarah Diaz and her staff warmly welcome visitors to this free house.

Real ales dispensed on handpump include Fremlins Bitter and a regularly changing stronger brew, such as Youngs Winter Warmer, Morland Old Speckled Hen or Adnams Extra. Also Boddingtons or Brakspear Mild.

The standard bar menu is chalked up on a blackboard above the bar and lists filled baked potatoes, ham, egg and chips, crofters lunch, Endeavour burger and fries, freshly-cut sandwiches and a choice of salads, such as quiche, ham, cheddar or Stilton. The adjacent dining room menu features grilled plaice, Dover Sole, chicken Kiev, steaks and duck with various sauces and is supplemented with a short selection of home-cooked weekend specials, for example, salmon and halibut en croûte, prawns in filo pastry, chilli and local game dishes. In summer the specials are available all the time. Puddings range from lemon meringue and chocolate roulade to home-made ice cream and hearty fruit pies and crumbles.

Weekday opening times are from 11am till 3pm and 6.30pm till 11pm.

Well behaved children are welcome inside. Dogs must be kept on a lead.

Telephone: (0303) 83268.

Walk No. 39

Village signposted off the A260 Folkestone road, 1½ miles south of the A2 at Denton.

Approx. distance of walk: 5 miles. O.S. Map No. 189 TR 223/465

There is a car park at the pub.

A peaceful farmland ramble on gently undulating field paths and established tracks. Generally easy going, but some tracks can be muddy underfoot. Of interest nearby is the Butterfly Centre at Swingfield Minnis (south on A260), where a tropical greenhouse garden features scores of colourful free-flying butterflies from all over the world (open Easter to early October).

1. Leave the pub, turn left along the quiet village lane, pass the Old Vicarage and take the waymarked hedged path left, just beyond house called Beamont. Climb a stile, proceed across a paddock to a further stile, then bear slightly right across pasture to a stile visible in the tree-lined hedgerow. Bear diagonally left on defined path through an open field towards a barn. Cross a stile, head half-right uphill to a stile, farm track and barn. Go through the gate opposite, bear half-left across pasture to the perimeter fence, then follow the fence left-handed to a stile in the field corner. Keep left along field edge beside woodland and shortly descend to a stile and lane.

2. Cross over, disregard the arrowed track right and follow the signed path ahead which soon bears diagonally left uphill across a field. At the field edge, keep right to a stile, proceed across paddock to another stile and shortly turn left along the footway beside the A260 at Selsted. Just beyond the Chequers pub cross over onto the opposite footway, then on passing a bungalow called Crosswinds turn right along a waymarked stony bridleway. Gently descend through woodland, then when the path bears sharp left into the wood, keep right onto a track

and head uphill on the woodland fringe to a gate. Follow field-edge right-handed to a metal gate, then head diagonally left across pasture to a wooden gate. Proceed along the grassy left-hand edge of a field to a stile flanking a gateway and join a lane.

3. Turn right along the lane, descend steeply to a road junction at the bottom of the hill and turn right onto the concrete drive to Rakeshole Farm. Keep to the grass-centred track to the right of the farm and maintain this valley bottom course on the well worn track for a mile before joining a driveway at Gatteridge Farm. Continue, pass Tappington Hall on your right to a lane. Turn right and follow it to the A260.

4. Cross straight over onto a defined earth track and gently ascend to the edge of Denton churchyard. Turn left along field edge, pass the church gate then shortly bear right off the grassy path to cross the driveway to Denton Court via two metal kissing gates. Proceed uphill through pasture, turn right beyond garden fence on your right and gradually bear left up the valley side towards the house on the woodland fringe and cross a metal ladder stile onto a lane. Turn right into Wootton, following the lane back to the pub.

The Tickled Trout, Wye

This neat, white-painted riverside building dates from about 1650 when it was used as a tannery and barges on the adjacent River Stour transported the 'cured' skins to the ports. It became an inn during the Victorian era and was called the Queen Victoria or the Old Vic to the locals and visitors to the now abandoned Wye racecourse. During the 1970's it closed, the building soon becoming almost derelict. Since then it has been given a new lease of life, capitalising on its attractive riverside setting and acquiring its present name from a tributary trout stream of the Great Stour. The pub has been smartly refurbished in modern 'rustic' style with exposed brickwork, dark wood-panelled walls, stained glass panels, old beams, shelves of old bottles, jars, china, books and nick-nacks and a comfortable mix of modern pine tables, captains chairs and padded wall bench seating. Delightful light and airy conservatory with floral curtains, cane furniture and views across the waterside lawn to the ancient stone bridge. The pub is a popular free house, especially in the summer, and is owned by Frank Wass, but efficiently run by Winston and Marie Legg.

On draught are Flowers Original, Fremlins Bitter, Boddingtons Bitter and Marstons Pedigree. Also available is the local farm cider - Theobalds Strong.

Good lunchtime bar food is listed on a printed menu and includes filling snacks - filled jacket potatoes, sandwiches, ploughmans, fresh salads - and hot dishes like steak, kidney and mushroom pie, supreme of chicken, cottage pie, chilli and a home-made soup. The evening menu changes every two weeks and may offer fresh tomato and pearl barley soup, garlic mushrooms and country pâté to start, followed by fillet of beef with a mushroom and Madeira sauce, turkey and ham pie, duck with orange sauce, steaks and not surprisingly 'tickled' trout with almonds. Both menus are supplemented by a few daily specials. To finish try the Kentish apple pie, sponge pudding or sherry trifle. Food is served daily from 12 noon till 2pm and 6pm till 9.30pm (till 10pm Friday and Saturday).

Weekday opening times are from 10.30am till 2.30pm and 6pm till 11pm. Open all day on summer Saturdays and till 3.30pm on Sundays in July and August.

Children are made very welcome. No dogs.

Telephone: (0233) 812227.

Walk No. 40

Wye is situated 1 mile off the A28, 3 miles north-east of Ashford.

Approx. distance of walk: 4¾ miles. O.S. Map No. 189 TQ 049/469.

The pub has a car park and parking is available at the Village Hall along the street.

A most enjoyable and scenic ramble across the Wye Downs with superb views across the eastern Weald and Romney Marsh. The walk explores Wye Down Nature Reserve and returns along well waymarked field paths and tracks. There is one steep climb to the top of the North Downs.

1. From the pub turn left along the main village street, then turn left into Church Street and shortly cross Churchfield Way into the churchyard. Bear diagonally right with North Downs Way marker along a tarmac path, then bear left between allotments and Wye College buildings. Pass round the back of the college onto a road, then cross a further road following the North Downs Way fingerpost. Follow the college road, pass through a metal gate at its end onto a wide track towards the Downs. Cross a lane and head uphill to a gate preceeding woodland.
2. Proceed steeply uphill on a narrow fenced path through trees to reach a lane. Turn right, gradually climb uphill, then cross a stile on your right and keep ahead to a stile beside a gate. Cross a further stile and turn left along the crest of the Downs, passing the crown shaped monument etched into the chalk hillside. Continue along the left-hand fence with magnificent views to a gate and a metalled driveway.
3. Turn right, cross a road and stile into Wye Downs National Nature Reserve. Follow the

waymarked path onto Broad Down, cross a stile and shortly turn right through a small wooden gate. Proceed along a grassy path to the edge of the Downs and descend on a chalky zig-zag path, crossing two stiles to a lane.
4. Turn right, then in a few yards climb a stile on your left and proceed straight ahead across an open field to a waymarked stile. Keep left-handed on a grassy path, pass through a gateway, then bear left through a second gateway and turn right with yellow marker along the right-hand edge of a field to a stile. Maintain direction, cross another stile beside a gate and follow the trackway to a further two stiles and cross a farm driveway. Climb a stile and continue along a track to a metalled lane and soon to pass Withersdane Hall on your right. Bear off left and join a narrow path beside playing fields, then cross a road onto a lane between houses back to the main village road. Turn left through the village back to the pub.

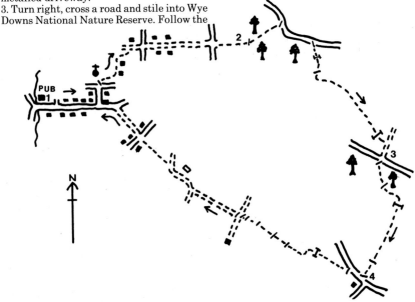

96